GUIDE TO OPERA & DANCE ON VIDEOCASSETTE

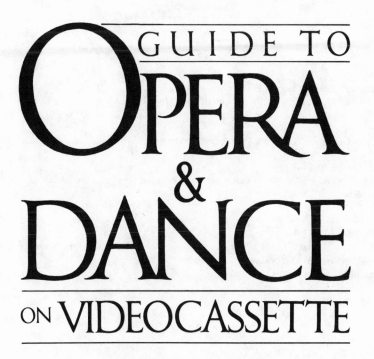

GUIDE TO
OPERA
&
DANCE
ON VIDEOCASSETTE

Robert Levine
and the Editors of
Consumer Reports Books

CONSUMERS UNION
Mount Vernon, New York

Copyright © 1989 by Robert Levine
Published by Consumers Union of United States, Inc., Mount Vernon, New York 10553.
All rights reserved, including the right of reproduction in whole or in part in any form.

Library of Congress Cataloging-in-Publication Data

Levine, Robert, 1944–
    Guide to opera and dance on videocassette / Robert Levine and the editors of Consumer
Reports Books.
        p. cm.
    Includes index.
    ISBN 0-89043-261-9
    1. Operas—Film and video adaptations—Reviews.   2. Ballets—Film and video adapta-
tions—Reviews.   3. Videocassettes—Reviews.
I. Consumer Reports Books.   II. Title.
ML1700.L49   1989
792.5'45—dc20   88-71036
                                                                                                      CIP
                                                                                                      MN

Design by Tamara O'Bradovich

First printing, December 1989
Manufactured in the United States of America

Guide to Opera and Dance on Videocassette is a Consumer Reports Book published by Consumers Union, the nonprofit organization that publishes *Consumer Reports*, the monthly
magazine of test reports, product Ratings, and buying guidance. Established in 1936, Consumers Union is chartered under the Not-For-Profit Corporation Law of the State of New
York.

    The purposes of Consumers Union, as stated in its charter, are to provide consumers with
information and counsel on consumer goods and services, to give information on all matters
relating to the expenditure of the family income, and to initiate and to cooperate with individual and group efforts seeking to create and maintain decent living standards.

    Consumers Union derives its income solely from the sale of *Consumer Reports* and other
publications. In addition, expenses of occasional public service efforts may be met, in part,
by nonrestrictive, noncommercial contributions, grants, and fees. Consumers Union accepts
no advertising or product samples and is not beholden in any way to any commercial interest. Its Ratings and reports are solely for the use of the readers of its publications. Neither
the Ratings nor the reports nor any Consumers Union publications, including this book, may
be used in advertising or for any commercial purpose. Consumers Union will take all steps
open to it to prevent such uses of its materials, its name, or the name of *Consumer Reports*.

BOMC offers recordings and compact discs, cassettes
and records. For information and catalog write to
BOMR, Camp Hill, PA 17012.

Contents

Acknowledgments

I would like to thank the following for their time, energy, patience, wisdom, advice, and assistance in the making of this book: James Seetoo, Kitty Benedict, Sam Shirakawa, Rosalie Muskatt, Sandi Gelles-Cole, and Julie Henderson.

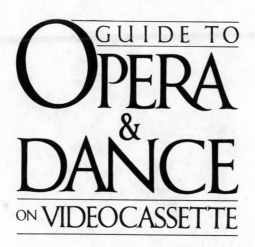

GUIDE TO OPERA & DANCE ON VIDEOCASSETTE

Introduction

It is said that Enrico Caruso made the phonograph popular; it is equally true that the phonograph made Caruso a household name. The early recordings of Caruso, despite their tinny sound and extraneous background noises, still fascinate new generations of opera lovers. Listeners sense, through the distortions of voice and instruments, a presence, a spontaneity, that is often lacking in today's overengineered recordings.

Television, in its early days, gave us glimpses of live (and lively) opera and dance before taping and prerecorded sound took over. Many of us can recall sitting before a tiny flickering TV screen, staring raptly at poorly staged opera vignettes, mediocre ballet "turns," or static orchestral pieces, just for the sheer novelty of having it all happen in our living room.

Like television, the invention and proliferation of VCRs and videotapes have led to a revolution in home musical entertainment. Tapes of performances featuring today's great singers and dancers are finding a place in neighborhood video stores and are attracting a much wider audience than Caruso, for one, ever dreamed was possible. And some of that vanished sense of immediacy has been recaptured in tapes of live opera and dance productions, filmed on stage as they actually happened.

Successfully filming opera and ballet, however, is a tricky business; often the taping of a live performance doesn't work as well as was hoped. Reducing an opera or ballet to a 19-inch (or smaller) TV screen presents a real challenge to directors and viewers alike, and even the best stage productions can look cramped and artificial on television.

Often, too, physical details that escape the notice of the theatre audience are only too apparent to the concentrated gaze of the home viewer. Inappropriate costumes, a performer's inadvertent grimaces or awkwardnesses, or a set designer's eccentricities can distract greatly, sometimes to the detriment of the performance itself.

The truth is that classical music on videocassette demands (as popular music has long since found out) a more imaginative approach, one that offers convincing characters and dramatic action or scenes that in turn enhance the music. This book is a testimony to the fact that it can be done, and done very successfully, whether as an original film or as a televised tape of a staged opera, ballet or concert performance.

This is not to deny that attending a live stage performance is preferable to watching a film, however varied and dramatic. No mechanical device can duplicate the excitement, the true-to-life sound, or the immediacy of the theatre. But the convenience and comfort of seeing your favorite opera or ballet at home is not to be scoffed at. You have the best seats in the house, intermissions at your whim, and the peace and quiet of your own home. More important, you can repeat the great moments of a particular performance, not only for yourself, but for your friends and family as well.

Videocassettes, then, must be seen in historical context, as part of a popular art that began with Caruso and the 78 RPM recording. Opera, as well as the dance, has especially profited from the videocassette revolution.

Opera on Videocassette

If any art form has been pulled, kicking and screaming, into the modern age, it is opera. In the process, it has had to discard many cherished shibboleths, among them antiquated acting techniques and the use of physically unsuited singers in leading romantic roles. Over the last few decades, at least, these common targets of popular humor are no longer the norm on the operatic stage.

If things are changing at the opera house, the small screen reflects an even deeper metamorphosis. We are now seeing singers who can look the part and act convincingly, and it's evident that such singers will be in great demand in the future. This fact has not been lost on young singers, for whom the craft of acting is now as important as voice production and training.

Another individual also plays an important role in the successful transfer of opera to film. The television director must work with—or, in many cases, around—the stage director in order to deal with a medium that shrinks the scene and cramps the action. At the same time the TV director must take advantage of the camera's ability to zero in and focus on a face or on an individual action.

There are problems as well. Where should the camera focus in an ensemble number, when the same words are repeated over and over? What about gaping mouths, bobbing tongues, surreptitious glances at the conductor or prompter? Opera in a huge theatre, such as the 25,000-seat Arena di Verona, presents other difficulties, including overacting, confused crowd scenes, and an inevitable blurring of the action. If the director has the imagination and experience to solve these problems, then the viewer will indeed have the best seat in the house.

Opera on videocassette gives the TV audience the great advantage of subtitles, which can explain a complicated plot, enhance understanding of the characters and their motives, and heighten enjoyment of the music itself. Many viewers find subtitles indispensable to their enjoyment of an opera on television.

Opera performances make up most of the entries in this volume. This is not surprising, since opera is meant to be seen as well as heard and is an international musical form that travels well. Today, by means of videocassettes, opera lovers can see operas as they are performed at La Scala, Glyndebourne, Verona, Covent Garden, and the Metropolitan Opera. They can enjoy their favorite operas, as well as rarely performed works, most of them featuring top singers and directors.

Besides full-length operas, fans can see and hear their favorite singers in recitals and concerts, and many fine documentaries are available on outstanding contemporary performers. Operatic parody and satire, as well as dramatizations of the lives of the composers, are also available on videocassette. Not all of these presentations are equally interesting, but almost all are worth watching at least once. And there's more coming out all the time.

Dance and Concerts on Videocassette

Video is also a boon to the balletomane, since dance is an ephemeral art and can be frozen in time only by means of film. And dance videocassettes offer many advantages: the film can be slowed down or speeded up, and a step can be replayed over and over again. One can see exactly how a difficult jump was executed, count the beats in an entrechat, admire the stunning height achieved in a grand jeté, study the mechanics of a graceful lift. If the performance is intelligently directed and filmed, the dancers can be seen from dramatically telling angles, so we don't miss facial expressions, gestures of mime, or other nuances often lost to the theater audience. The small screen may fail to encompass the sense of spatial patterning achieved in stage productions, but the viewer's eye adapts quickly to this limitation and compensates in other ways for such distortions.

Videocassettes also enable one to see those legendary dancers never before seen in the West. Dance tapes allow us to compare dancers and techniques, analyze the work of famous choreographers, and see individual pieces that are performed only in their native countries. The videocassette is our ticket to a world of dance.

Instrumental or orchestral programs, on the other hand, tend to be less visually gripping on the small screen. No matter how worthwhile their musical content, endless shots of violinists bowing or horns blowing can make even the most musical viewer yawn in boredom. And, obviously, any visual criticism is redundant and unnecessary. For this reason, concerts on videocassette have received the least space in this volume.

Instead, we have confined ourselves to the few available tapes of the great musicians of the past—Toscanini, Arrau, Horowitz, Heifetz—plus three extraordinary series that combine great music with much visually interesting material: *Guitarra!* with Julian Bream, *The Story of the Symphony* with André Previn, and *The Music of Man* with Yehudi Menuhin. All of these multicassette series contain lengthy concert segments, but more important, they offer an absorbing and enlightening view of the history of music. They are also handsomely produced and, in addition to their entertainment value, are excellent learning tools for young and not-so-young alike.

The videos reviewed in this volume do not include every concert, opera, or dance tape on the market today. We have reviewed a cross section of repertory staples, some rarities, a number of TV documentaries and specials, and a few feature films. The staples, whether of opera or ballet, are generally available in video outlet stores that carry a large selection; this volume is especially helpful in choosing between two or more performances of the same work. The rarities may be specialty items of interest to the aficionado or gems that deserve more attention. If these particular tapes are not readily available, contact the production companies and distributors listed in the appendix for purchasing information.

In the lists of credits for each work, television directors, set designers, and costumers are noted only when a specific point is made about their contributions. Minor cast members in operas, or second and third soloists in ballets, are mentioned only if their work is exceptional in one way or another.

About 90 percent of the operas available on videocassette are subtitled in English. Make certain you get the version you want before purchasing or renting. The picture and sound quality on all tapes reviewed is good to excellent unless otherwise noted.

A word about the evaluations in this book. Each review is based on the author's musical knowledge and critical expertise, plus a deep familiarity with most of the works mentioned here, both on stage and on videocassette. Doubtless, not all readers will agree with our judgment. The VCR, however, allows us to make our own comparisons and evaluations whenever desirable or necessary.

This book is intended to furnish a basis for making an intelligent selection in the classical music videocassette marketplace. Videocassettes are expensive to buy, if not to rent, and the decision to purchase depends on whether one wants an evening's entertainment or a lifelong possession. This book tells what is available, what to expect for the money, and what performances stand up to repeated viewings. Because prices and discount practices vary widely, they have not been provided here.

The reader should be aware that manufacturers may temporarily withdraw certain videocassettes from the market. But, like out-of-print books, they are often made available again, sometimes from a different distributor, or from several new distributors.

The number of listings in this book is a welcome indication that opera and dance on videocassette are now a significant segment of the home entertainment market. And there are more coming out all the time.

ONE

OPERA ON VIDEOCASSETTE

Opera: Stage Productions

▇ Handel: *Agrippina*

Barbara Daniels, Gunter von Kannen, David Kuebler, Janice Hall, Claudio Nicolai, Carlos Feller, other soloists; The London Baroque Players, Arnold Östman, cond. A production of the Schwetzingen Festival.

Home Vision, color, 1985, 160 minutes. Italian with English subtitles.

Agrippina was first performed in 1709 and ran for twenty-seven nights—quite a hit by Baroque standards. The Machiavellian plot involves the scheming wife of Claudius and mother of Nero, who attempts to get her son on the Roman throne upon hearing false reports of Claudius' death. The opera has a rich libretto by Vincenzo Grimani and is filled with drama and some of Handel's most colorful music. It also offers a cast of classically corrupt Romans, who somehow manage to wind up happy in the end.

The main problem with this Schwetzingen Festival production is that the orchestral and vocal elements are not at one. Arnold Östman, one of the finest conductors in the authentic instrument movement (he's music director of Sweden's Drottningholm Court Theatre) leads the London Baroque Players on original instruments. They play with light touch and texture, no rubato, and just the right Baroque ornamentation. The singers, on the other hand, are conventional, with rich voices full of vibrato, a no-no in Baroque works. In Handel's original casting, the role of Nerone was sung by a soprano castrato, Ottone by a female contralto, and Narciso by an alto castrato. Here Nero could have—should have—been

9

sung by a countertenor, as should Narciso. Instead, the roles are given to tenors, and Ottone is sung by a basso-buffo.

David Kuebler, the Nerone, has an agile, well-focused lyric voice that can handle the role's difficulties, but for the most part he sings an octave lower than he should. His performance is good, but the characterization is essentially wrong. The same is true for Ottone. Claudio Nicolai's unattractive buffo voice is not agile enough for the music: he's short of breath and has little command of the idiom. The Narciso is foolish as well, but much of his role is cut. Carlos Feller makes the most of the role of Lesbo.

The interesting character bass Gunter von Kannen knows his way around the music but plays Claudius as an old windbag, which is disconcerting. Janice Hall's Poppea is wonderful—self-centered, sexy, and tonally alluring. But the real star is Barbara Daniels, whose Agrippina is near-perfect. Her bright, shiny voice copes well with the fiendishly difficult music, and she moves and acts well. She seems to take the audience into her confidence, and we side with her. In the end, she either gives in to effect a compromise or is defeated by Claudius' stupidity, generosity, or genius—it's not all that clear.

However much one may disagree with director Michael Hampe's conception of the roles, he certainly proves the stageworthiness of this opera. Mauro Pagano's sets are handsome. Thomas Olofsson's direction for television is ideal: he understands the artificial, classic idiom and weds it to modern technology without a hitch.

Overall, despite the lack of authenticity caused by some of the director's casting choices, this production is a treat.

■ Cilea: *Adriana Lecouvreur*

Joan Sutherland, Heather Begg, Anson Austin, John Shaw, others; the Australian Opera Chorus and the Elizabethan Sydney Orchestra, Richard Bonynge, cond. Directed by John Copley; designed by Allan Lees and Michael Stennett.

Sony, color, 1984, 135 minutes. Italian with English subtitles.

Adriana Lecouvreur is a favorite showcase for some sopranos and for many opera lovers. The title character is an actress, whom we observe at her most dramatic—reciting lines in reverie, declaiming in anger, rhapsodizing in a state of hallucination. The role lies comfortably in the middle voice, and the heroine has two beautiful arias, plus a fifteen-minute death scene. The tenor role, meant for a real *spinto*, is a beauty as well, and even the mezzo has her moments. In other words, the opera (however sentimental the plot) contains all the ingredients of a success. This particular performance, however, is a near failure.

Joan Sutherland is badly miscast in the title role, which requires exclamatory ability and good acting—not her strong points. But she does as well as she can, using the hollow bottom of her voice with drama, articulating well, and moving with ease. One expects a coloratura riff to peal forth, but in vain. As good as she is, even *La Stupenda*'s greatest fans will be disappointed; this is just not the role for her.

The tenor Anson Austin, her presumably ardent lover Maurizio, is also in the wrong opera. He has a nice, light voice but can't convey the heroic style needed here. Heather Begg is far from good as the wicked Principessa di Bouillon, though she throws herself into the role with energy and enthusiasm. John Shaw is a good Michonnet.

Richard Bonynge's conducting is too fast, too light, and generally too flippant for this melodramatic opera. The sets and costumes are beautiful, and John Copley's direction would make sense if only the singers were up to their roles.

■ Verdi: *Aïda*

Maria Chiara, Fiorenza Cossotto, Nicola Martinucci, Giuseppe Scandola, Carlo Zardo; Chorus, Orchestra and Corps de Ballet of the Arena di Verona, Anton Guadagno, cond.

HBO Video, color, 1981, 150 minutes. Italian with English subtitles.

Aïda is the perfect opera for the 25,000-seat Arena di Verona. This production particularly plays on the work's grandiose setting, emphasizing the spectacle in hopes that the intimate moments will take care of themselves. The handsome sets and costumes are by Vittorio Rossi, and the production seemingly comprises a cast of thousands.

Maria Chiara, a soprano too often ignored on this side of the Atlantic, sings a well-conceived, controlled, elegant Aïda. Her acting has Theda Bara overtones, but no one seems to mind. Cossotto's familiar Amneris is a towering characterization, and her judgment scene is overwhelmingly intense. Allowing her to fully let out her huge voice agrees with her; there's none of her customary flatting above the staff. Nicola Martinucci is a Verona favorite, and his Radames cuts a fine-looking figure with plenty of voice if not much subtlety. Giuseppe Scandola gives a noisy, insensitive performance as Amonasro.

The gold-and-ivory triumphal scene is as effective as the bathed-in-blue Nile act. The intelligent camerawork is a distinct asset: it assures that the home viewer will see the details that at least 20,000 of those in the Arena are missing. Guadagno leads sympathetically and with verve, although he takes the final duet too fast. In short, not an *Aïda* for the ages (or even the best available), but still a good evening's entertainment.

▮ Verdi: *Aïda*

Maria Chiara, Ghena Dimitrova, Luciano Pavarotti, Juan Pons, Nicolai Ghiaurov, Paata Burchuladze, other soloists; Orchestra and Chorus of La Scala, Milan, Lorin Maazel, cond.

Home Vision, color, 1986, 160 minutes. Italian with English subtitles.

The main problems with this production of *Aïda* are the inappropriate sets and costumes. Designer Mauro Pagano has confusingly set the first two acts on vast, ugly plains (on which mysterious buildings go up as we watch) and then, in the last two acts, gives us sets that are both realistic and handsome. Meanwhile, the costumer refuses to acknowledge any particular season of the year, makes Pavarotti look more enormous than he already is, and forces Maria Chiara, the Aïda, to wear a ridiculous piece of headgear in the last scene. Luca Ronconi's direction, too, is frequently pointless and silly. Remarkably, none of these visual or dramatic errors gets in the way of the music—quite a testimony to the high level of vocal and orchestral musicianship.

A surprise piece of casting finds dramatic soprano Ghena Dimitrova in the mezzo role of Amneris, and it works. True, one occasionally misses the heavy chest tones a mezzo brings to the part, but Dimitrova's piercing, secure top and fine grasp of the drama make her Amneris a believable and sometimes frightening character. Pavarotti is vocally breathtaking as Radames, despite a rushed "Celeste Aïda." The voice itself is, of course, magnificent, but he also amazes with the power he brings to the part. Maria Chiara is never less than good in the title role, and is occasionally inspired to near-greatness. She hasn't learned to act since the earlier, Verona performance, but it hardly matters. Vocally, Ghiaurov is a bit too old to sing Ramfis, but Paata Burchuladze, a young Soviet bass, makes a splendid video debut as the King. Juan Pons's voice lacks the shine

Amonasro needs but his reading is so insightful that he's thoroughly convincing.

The show's real star may just be Lorin Maazel, who gives an enlightening account of the score. Strings shimmer, woodwinds haunt and insinuate, brass makes the needed effect. The singers interact under his leadership to create real drama—a case in point is the first act Aïda-Radames-Amneris trio.

And so, sit back and enjoy a finely performed Aïda—just laugh at the sets, costumes, and direction. Highly recommended.

■ Britten: *Albert Herring*

John Graham-Hall, Patricia Johnson, Alan Opie, Felicity Palmer, Elizabeth Gale, Richard van Allan, other soloists; the Glyndebourne Chorus, Soloists of the London Philharmonic Orchestra, Bernard Haitink, cond.

Home Vision, color, 1985, 145 minutes. English.

We're fortunate to have this gem available on videocassette—and in such near-perfect form. Directed for the stage and TV by Peter Hall and Robin Lough, this video is a must for those who admire this 1947 comic bauble (Britten was never to be in such a mood again). It's an ideal way for the uninitiated to get to know the opera as well.

Based on a story by Guy de Maupassant, *Albert Herring* is an exquisitely astute portrait of small-town provincialism. Unable to find a suitable virgin to be crowned May Queen, the pillars of the community choose the mama's boy Albert Herring to be their May King. He gets tipsy at his coronation and disappears for a night of debauchery. When he returns, he tells off the self-righteous snobs of the town. It is an impeccable social comedy, with no minor characters, and great economy of musical composition; only a chamber orchestra is used, but to great effect. Moreover, this Glyndebourne production, designed by John Gunter, is as good to look at as it is to hear.

At the opera's core is Patricia Johnson's portrayal of Lady Billows, surely one of the greatest bullies in opera. In the role she snubs everyone with a vengeance and handles the heroic vocal demands with ease. Felicity Palmer sings and acts Lady Billows's maid, Florence, with just the right whining outrage, aided and abetted by Elizabeth Gale as Miss Wordsworth and Richard van Allan as Police Superintendent Budd. Alan Opie and Jean Rigby sing Sid and Nancy—the couple who spike Albert's punch and get the trouble going—and they're a delight.

In the title role, John Graham-Hall is no simpering dolt but, rather, a lad who grasps the opportunity to break out with both hands. The tenor has a fine voice and a wonderfully innocent face. Conductor Haitink clearly loves this score, and he invites us in on the fun. The engineers could have kept the orchestral sound down so we could better discern the words, but it is nice to hear the instrumentation with such clarity.

In short, this is a delight. Heartily recommended.

◼ Giordano: *Andrea Chenier*

José Carreras, Eva Marton, Piero Cappuccilli, Nella Verri, other soloists; Orchestra and Chorus of La Scala, Milan, Riccardo Chailly, cond.

Home Vision, color, 1985, 130 minutes. Italian with English subtitles.

"The best of the B operas" is how *Andrea Chenier* is described in some circles. Although the opera lacks substance, it does have lots of Italianate emotional fireworks, some beautiful melodies, and grand dramatic climaxes. It also needs at least two or three great singers to do it justice. This handsome production, taped at La Scala in 1985, is pleasing to the eye (the costumes are all in French Revolutionary reds, whites, and blues), and director Lamberto Puggelli manages to convey a sense of a becalmed and ignorant aristocracy amid a simmering, discontented populace. Brian Large, directing for television, keeps the camera focused on the action.

All of the performances are good, but, unfortunately, none is really great. José Carreras's voice is too light for the title role and he sometimes strains; his intelligence, ardor, and handsome appearance almost make up for his vocal shortcomings. Eva Marton has a different problem with her large voice: in the big scenes she's quite thrilling but has trouble scaling her voice down in Maddalena's quieter, more girlish moments. Baritone Piero Cappuccilli has the voice and the temperament for Carlo Gerard but offers no insights into this, the opera's only really conflicted character. Nella Verri is a fine, spiteful Countess, and the rest of the cast is adequate.

Chailly conducts as if this were very important music indeed, and he keeps the chaotic second and third act ensembles together impressively. (He would have been wise to give Carreras more breadth in his first-act aria, but he apparently chose not to.) The La Scala forces play well; for once the opera's finale does not sound as if it were scored for clashing garbage can lids. This tape is not wholeheartedly recommended, but it's worth seeing and hearing, at least once.

■ Giordano: *Andrea Chenier*

Mario del Monaco, Antonietta Stella, Giuseppe Taddei, Orchestra and Chorus of RAI, Angelo Questa, cond.

Lyric Distribution, black & white, 1958, 116 minutes. Italian, no subtitles.

The picture quality of this old movie is a bit murky, but not enough to put you off. Del Monaco was a great Chenier, with just the right trumpetlike quality needed to carry his role. He's also in one of his sensitive, poetic moods here, and so his is a totally successful performance, full of both feeling and ringing tone. Antonietta Stella, a fine soprano who was rarely moved to great heights, is at her best here as Maddalena. Though there isn't much depth to her reading, her third act aria is delivered as well as you're likely to hear it.

The finest moments, however, come from baritone Giuseppe Taddei as Carlo Gerard. Malevolent and moving, he electrifies every scene he's in, making us totally believe in this servant-turned-revolutionary.

The production (on stage, with no audience, and lip-synched) is attractive, the direction intelligent. Angelo Questa is an able conductor, moving at a brisk pace and keeping the big ensembles together. This is an interesting document and a good show to boot.

■ Strauss: *Arabella*

Ashley Putnam, Gianna Rolandi, Regina Sarfaty, John Bröcheler, Artur Korn, Keith Lewis, Gwendolyn Bradley; the London Philharmonic Orchestra and Glyndebourne Festival Chorus, Bernard Haitink, cond.

HBO Video, color, 1984, 154 minutes. German with English subtitles.

The only undisputed star of this performance is the London Philharmonic Orchestra, which here plays brilliantly for Maestro Haitink. All of Strauss's lovely woodwind writing comes through clearly and with purity of tone, and the opera moves at a brisk pace. John Cox, too, is to be praised for his direction, as is Julia Trevelyan Oman for her evocative sets and costumes. Sadly, the singing is not up to the level of the orchestral playing, conducting, or production.

Ashley Putnam, in the title role, looks beautiful and sings well enough, but never reaches the dramatic or vocal heights that the role demands. Arabella's sister Zdenka is sung by Gianna Rolandi, and although she acts with impulsive authority, the effort apparent in the production of her upper voice is a great deterrent to our enjoyment. Baritone John Bröcheler makes little of Mandryka's music or personality—his light voice is forced beyond its limits, even in a house as small as Glyndebourne, and his acting is stiff. Regina Sarfaty and Artur Korn impress as the girls' parents, and Keith Lewis as Matteo and Gwendolyn Bradley as the Fiakermilli (the silliest role for coloratura soprano in all of opera) are excellent.

Arabella is long on conversation and when the music does take flight— as in the sisters' first-act duet, the second-act duet between Arabella and Mandryka, and Arabella's final scene—it needs great singing to make it soar. Sadly, it's all a bit earthbound here. Acceptable if you must own an *Arabella*, but little more.

◼ Verdi: *Attila*

Yevgeny Nesterenko, Maria Chiara, Silvano Carroli, Veriano Luchetti; Chorus and Orchestra of the Arena di Verona, Nello Santi, cond.

Home Vision, color, 1985, 120 minutes. Italian with English subtitles.

This is Verdi's ninth opera and no one's favorite. Much of it makes little sense dramatically (the eponymous Hun turns out to be not so bad after all), and the music is almost never memorable. Nor does the work point toward the composer's later masterpieces; in some ways it is a throwback to what Verdi referred to as his "galley days." Still, its lack of subtlety makes listening and watching it such fun, and despite some problems this tape is worth viewing.

The fact that the opera is here performed complete, with all repeats in the arias and cabalettas, must be applauded. Since we probably won't see another version on tape for some time, this one will have to stand as a historical document as well. The production at the Arena di Verona is typically overwhelming in its scope; when a flock of doves is released at the close of the first act, we know that the opera has found its true home.

Yevgeny Nesterenko sings Attila with rolling tones and surprisingly good Italian diction. He also looks comfortable on a horse, which seems to matter in this production. His duet with Silvano Carroli, which closes the first scene of the prologue (this oddly constructed work has a prologue that takes up more than a third of the opera), shows off both voices to full advantage and brings the house down. Carroli, with his burly voice, is equally effective in his second-act scene, displaying no great interpretive insights but plenty of sheer sound. Veriano Luchetti tries hard as Foresto, the tenor hero, but his tone is unappealing.

Maria Chiara is Odabella, a difficult role. Soul sister to Verdi's Abigaille and Lady Macbeth, she has a first-act scene calling for soprano heroics. Chiara goes all out and sings on key often enough to please, but she's pushed to her limit here and sounds at times as if she's tempting fate. But there are plenty of thrills in her interpretation of the role, if you can relax long enough to sit back and listen.

Director Giuliano Montaldo has done an impressive job with an opera that needs little interpretation, but an intelligent performance, to make it worthwhile. Sets and costumes are properly lavish. Nello Santi, an underrated conductor, holds everything together, and the Verona orchestra and chorus play and sing with genuine fervor. The picture and sound are particularly good.

A must for Verdi specialists.

■ Verdi: *Un Ballo in Maschera*

Katia Ricciarelli, Luciano Pavarotti, Bianca Berini, Louis Quilico, Judith Blegen, others; Metropolitan Opera Orchestra and Chorus, Giuseppe Patané, cond. Directed by Elijah Moshinsky.

Paramount Home Video, color, 1980, 150 minutes. Italian with English subtitles.

This production of *Un Ballo in Maschera* is staged in colonial Boston, but designer Peter Wexler's unorthodox ideas are out of place in that milieu. The first act is set in what looks like a huge gymnasium with chandeliers and a pool table, and the second act "gallows" scene contains a balcony and is particularly incomprehensible. By the time a traditional set is restored in the final act, it's too late. The stage is so severely raked that one fears for the singers' safety. Elijah Moshinsky's direction, too, is mysterious: Riccardo sings of his love for Amelia with everybody listening; he looks inappropriately terrified by Ulrica's prediction; Amelia lifts her own veil so that the conspirators and Renato can see who she really is; and there is some odd business going on in Ulrica's strangely elegant hut involving a brunette who is apparently possessed by the devil. This is a dramatically senseless *Ballo*, but much of the singing more than makes up for it.

Luciano Pavarotti's role suits him perfectly. He sings with great rhythmic accuracy; his tone is open, free, and beautiful; and he acts competently. Although he and the conductor are at odds in the second-act duet—and he wears a ludicrous wig—he is the right tenor for Riccardo. Katia Ricciarelli sounds better here than she has since, with only a few problems above the staff at *forte*. She looks radiant, acts convincingly, and sings a positively superb "Morrò, ma prima in grazia." She's not perfectly suited for the role of Amelia, however.

Louis Quilico, as Renato, is very good if a bit blustery. As usual, he works too hard and tends to remain very much himself instead of the character he's playing. Bianca Berini, dressed like a berserk pilgrim, is an imposing presence as Ulrica, without an imposing voice, although she is effective in the role. Judith Blegen chirps her way through Oscar's music, occasionally flying sharp. The oddly dressed conspirators are impressively menacing.

Giuseppe Patané's conducting is competent if not inspired. The Met Orchestra and Chorus are at their best (one wishes that the audience would not break into applause quite so often). But enough complaints—the music is well served and the tape is recommended.

■ Rossini: *The Barber of Seville*

Maria Ewing, Max-René Cosotti, John Rawnsley, Claudio Desderi, Ferruccio Furlanetto, soloists; The London Philharmonic Orchestra and Glyndebourne Festival Chorus, Sylvain Cambreling, cond.

Home Vision, color, 1982, 155 minutes. Italian with English subtitles.

Director John Cox has decided to dispense with much of the slapstick and vulgar tricks that are usually a part of this Rossini favorite. Instead, he creates a comedy of manners, pointing out the characters' eccentricities along the way. He is in agreement with both designer William Dudley, whose sets are whimsical and realistic, and conductor Sylvain Cambreling, who leads a thoughtful, musically accurate reading of the score.

Claudio Desderi and Ferruccio Furlanetto (*not* Curt Appelgren as the accompanying booklet announces) are a fine pair as a younger-than-usual Bartolo and Basilio. They manage Rossini's difficult vocal line with ease and create real, troublemaking characters. Tenor Max-René Cosotti, after a sloppy opening aria, settles into the role of the Count nicely, cutting a handsome figure and displaying a fine sense of comedy. The two other minor roles are adequately performed.

The two leads, Rosina and Figaro, fall to an American and an Englishman—proving that it's not necessary to be Italian to have a genuine Italian singing style. Maria Ewing, as the know-it-all Rosina, is in complete control. Her playing to the camera seems right, and she is more than equal to the vocal demands. Her ideas of the role are her own, and she looks as good as she sounds. John Rawnsley has some rough moments with Figaro's more florid music, but what baritone doesn't? His is a funny, classy performance.

Home Vision's recording was faintly out of sync in the second act (you may want to test it before investing), and the sound occasionally drops out for a split second. The subtitles are witty and enlightening.

Though far from perfect, this performance is worth it for the director's conception and for Maria Ewing's Rosina.

■ Gay: *The Beggar's Opera*

Roger Daltrey, Stratford Johns, Patricia Routledge, Carol Hall, Bob Hoskins, others; The English Baroque Soloists, John Eliot Gardiner, cond. Music arranged by Jeremy Barlow and John Eliot Gardiner. Produced and directed by Jonathan Miller.

Home Vision, color, 1983, 135 minutes. English.

John Gay's 1728 *The Beggar's Opera* is an opera only in the loosest sense. It is actually a ballad opera, a vernacular English form in which popular tunes of the day were dropped into a satirical play. In effect, it is far closer to *Of Thee I Sing* than to Handel's *Giulio Cesare*. A raging success when it first appeared, it has remained popular long enough to inspire the Brecht-Weill work *The Threepenny Opera*.

This 1983 BBC taping features a stellar production team and some exceptional performers. John Eliot Gardiner, one of the most respected names in the authentic performance movement, is the music director, and he has arranged the work's sixty-nine musical snippets with the assistance of Jeremy Barlow, whose Broadside Band is closely associated with this repertoire. (The work of John Pepusch, the original arranger, is rarely in evidence here.) The musicians are the wonderful English Baroque Soloists. The producer/director is that multitalented Renaissance man, Jonathan Miller, and the role of Macheath is acted and sung by Roger Daltrey of the great rock band The Who. In principle, then, this is a fabulous undertaking; in reality, the effect is somehow stultifying and unsatisfactory.

Perhaps we're living in the wrong century to enjoy an "authentic" performance of this work. What brought eighteenth-century audiences to their feet can all too easily strike us as merely quaint. The pace is tough to take; none of the sixty-nine pieces of music is longer than two minutes, and the work runs to over two hours. In addition, we can understand the accents of the players only about half the time. (The fine actor Bob Hoskins appears intermittently; at the start he is incomprehensible, at the close, perfectly easy to understand.) As a result we find ourselves working too hard and having too little fun. The handsome production isn't enough to make up for the yawning distance between the viewer and what the creators had in mind.

Musically, there is little to complain about. We will never know exactly what the audiences of the time heard (the music survives only as notated melodies, with no indication of instrumentation), but what Gardiner and Barlow have decided that we should hear is as good a guess as any and nicely performed. The instruments could have been more prominently recorded, but the decision to keep them in the background seems to have been deliberate.

Another minor problem is that the voices are not all of a type: Patricia Routledge, as Mrs. Peachum, for example, sounds like an opera singer, while Carol Hill's Polly is better suited to the folksy quality of the music (though she has a tough time with some of the trickier passages). The finest performance comes from Roger Daltrey as Macheath. Although he sometimes seems intimidated by the music, his voice suits the part and is dramatically convincing.

Jonathan Miller has somehow turned a work that was once riotously alive into a historical curiosity. This piece may be watched once with some pleasure, but it's unlikely anyone will want to see it again.

■ Puccini: *La Bohème*

Ileana Cotrubas, Marilyn Zschau, Neil Shicoff, Thomas Allen, John Rawnsley, Gwynne Howell, Brian Donlon, other soloists; Orchestra of the Royal Opera House, Covent Garden, the Royal Opera Chorus, Lamberto Gardelli, cond.

HBO Video, color, 1982, 115 minutes. Italian with English subtitles.

This is a good performance of *Bohème*, although it never reaches the inspired stage. One of the problems is the sound, which is a bit removed in the first two acts (mysteriously remedied, though, by the third). Another drawback is the lighting, which is too bright throughout. A third problem is the conducting of Lamberto Gardelli, which doesn't empha- size the more fun-loving moments in order to provide a contrast to the ultimate tragedy. Where the show does shine, however, is in the solo singing, which is for the most part on a very high level.

Cotrubas and Shicoff are sympathetic singing actors, and both are in fine voice. Shicoff is nicely impetuous and Cotrubas is delicate and girl- ish—only the close-ups reveal her age. Thomas Allen is a golden-toned Marcello, Gwynne Howell makes the most of Colline's last-act aria, and John Rawnsley treats Schaunard as if it were a leading role. The men actu- ally seem to be friends, and John Copley's direction is right on target. Marilyn Zschau's voice is too large for Musetta and tends to go off pitch, but she, too, enters into the spirit of the story. Julia Trevelyan Oman has created lovely, intimate sets (with some surprises in the second act) and handsome costumes. A well-sung and well-acted evening, but one that seems to lack sparkle, particularly compared with the Met-and-Zeffirelli staging.

■ Puccini: *La Bohème*

Teresa Stratas, Renata Scotto, José Carreras, Richard Stilwell, Allan Monk, James Morris, Italo Tajo, other soloists; Metropolitan Opera Orchestra and Chorus, James Levine, cond.

Paramount Home Video, color, 1982, 141 minutes (including 20- minute special: "Zeffirelli and *Bohème*"). Italian with English subtitles.

When *La Bohème* was premiered in 1896, with Arturo Toscanini conducting, the public took it immediately to its heart. The critics did not, however. Carlo Bersezio, Turin's most influential critic, predicted that the opera would "leave only a small impression in the history of our lyric theatre." Time has proved him abysmally wrong.

This production is by Franco Zeffirelli. When it first appeared at the Met (and since then, for that matter), critics condemned it as too big, too busy, too overwhelming. Happily, the advent of videocassettes remedies these faults. The camera makes the action clear at all times, and we are never in danger of misplacing the main characters, even during the wild second act, when there are close to 400 people on stage. The camera also helps to restore the story's intimate tone and lets us feel that we are looking at a slice of real Parisian life.

Ileana Cotrubas and Neil Shicoff in a scene from the Royal Opera production of Puccini's *La Bohème*. Photo by Catherine Ashmore. Courtesy HBO Video.

Teresa Stratas is at her most moving, and her combination of emotional strength and physical weakness is just right for Mimi. She is in far from perfect voice, but the genuine depth of feeling that she conveys more than makes up for an occasional strained tone. Her "Addio, senza rancor" in the third act is heartrending.

José Carreras, no less fine than Stratas, looks youthful and ardent and sounds for all the world like the poet Rodolfo he's portraying. He transposes his first-act aria down a semi-tone (as does almost every tenor singing the role today) and strains a bit at the top of his voice, but these are minor carpings.

The rest of the cast is almost uniformly excellent. Renata Scotto makes some occasionally overbearing sounds as Musetta, but her dramatic involvement is undeniable. Richard Stilwell exudes charm and sincerity as Marcello, Allan Monk sings beautifully as Schaunard, and James Morris is both moving and blustering as Colline. The wonderful thing about this presentation is its credibility. Much of the credit must go to James Levine for his understanding leadership, to Franco Zeffirelli for his sensitive direction of the intimate moments, and to TV director Kirk Browning for the brilliant camerawork. No video collection would be complete without this *Bohème*.

■ Mussorgsky: *Boris Godunov*

Yevgeny Nesterenko, Vladislav Piasko, Irina Arkhipova, Valery Yaroslavtsev, Artur Eisen, Galina Kalinina, Aleksei Maslennikov; Bolshoi Opera Chorus and Orchestra; Boris Khaikin, cond.

Kultur, color, 1978, stereo, 181 minutes. Russian with English subtitles.

This production has much to recommend it: the sets are huge and colorful, the chorus of the Bolshoi lives up to its legendary status, and there isn't a weak performance in the cast. The only cut is in the so-called Polish Act—about half of it has been excised and the role of the priest, Rangoni, has been eliminated. This is a customary cut but a regrettable one. Videocassettes are essentially historical documents and it would be valuable to see all of what Mussorgsky actually composed, complete, on his home ground.

Yevgeny Nesterenko's Boris is a towering characterization—a human being of great depth and complexity. Nesterenko's portrayal of the czar's inner torment and guilt is intensely moving, and his voice is an instrument of great beauty. Similarly, tenor Vladislav Piasko's false Dimitri is totally believable—a man of real flesh and blood. Valery Yaroslavtsev's Pimen is younger-sounding than usual, but his interpretation is well conceived and highly effective. Artur Eisen's Varlaam, on the other hand, though plentiful in voice, remains a shell. Irina Arkhipova's Marina, or what's left of her after the cuts, makes one miss the rest of her music. The rest of the cast is fine, with special praise reserved for Aleksei Maslennikov's Simpleton, whose laments are so beautifully sung that one feels intensely the sad plight of Mother Russia.

Boris Khaikin's control of the orchestra is masterful; he moves very little but gets grand playing from his small gestures. One could wish that the stage lighting weren't always so bright (perhaps this was done to accommodate the videotaping), but this is a quibble. Getting to see the quintessential Russian opera so well performed is enough. *Boris* fans should not miss this one.

■ Rossini: *La Cenerentola*

Kathleen Kuhlmann, Laurence Dale, Alberto Rinaldi, Claudio Desderi, Roderick Kennedy, Marta Taddei, Laura Zannini; the Glyndebourne Chorus and London Philharmonic Orchestra, Donato Renzetti, cond. Directed by John Cox, designed by Allen Charles Klein.

HBO Video, color, 1983, 152 minutes. Italian with English subtitles.

Rossini's Cinderella opera has come back into the repertory only in the past couple of decades. The reason for its previous obscurity is easy to understand: the right kinds of voices were not available to perform it successfully in the major opera houses. Only since Maria Callas almost single-handedly led the bel canto revival (later helped, of course, by Joan Sutherland, Beverly Sills, Marilyn Horne, and a few others) have people begun to look at this composer's more obscure operas. Rossini needs, above all, voices with great agility, and his highly decorated vocal lines demand clear articulation. The performance under consideration here actually boasts a group of singers who fill the bill.

Kathleen Kuhlmann is a mezzo-soprano with all the notes, a nice if not exceptional timbre, and a true sense of the style. She makes Cenerentola appealing without ever becoming maudlin, and some of her virtuosity is truly astonishing. She is badly costumed throughout, however. (All of the costumes are a horror to behold.) Her Prince (Ramiro), tenor Laurence Dale, looks about fifteen years old, is dressed and coiffed like a Gainsborough painting, and is not afraid of the role's high tessitura. His light voice deals well with the coloratura, without ever dazzling, and in all, his is a fine portrayal.

As Dandini, the Prince's valet (who is disguised as the Prince) baritone Alberto Rinaldi cannot quite cope with the music's demands and smudges some runs. But he has the right attitude and manages his opening aria with flair, even though he has to sing it atop a wooden horse. Claudio Desderi as Don Magnifico, Cenerentola's father, is fluent, biting, funny, and nasty all at once—he is a great singing actor. Roderick Kennedy sings Alidoro (Rossini's answer to the fairy godmother) with ease and a knowing smile. The rest of the cast, orchestra, and chorus perform admirably, and Donato Renzetti's leadership cannot be faulted.

Unfortunately, the physical production is fairy-tale storybook cute, and the scenery begins to cloy about halfway through the first act. John Cox's direction, though, keeps things moving gently and without exaggeration or vulgarity; and John Vernon, the director for television, is equally sensitive. This is a worthwhile performance of an unjustly neglected work and is to be recommended. Newcomers to this opera are in for some nice surprises.

▪ Mozart: *Cosi fan tutte*

Anne-Christine Biel, Maria Höglind, Ulla Severin, Lars Tibell, Magnus Linden, Enzo Florimo, soloists; the Orchestra and Chorus of the Drottningholm Court Theatre (Sweden), Arnold Östman, cond.

HBO Video, color, 1984, 141 minutes. Italian with English subtitles.

Although there is no legendary, showstopping, or even particularly memorable vocal performance in this production, it is one of the finest *Cosi*s produced in the last decade or so. Director Willy Decker's dark view of the work is backed up at every moment both by Mozart and his librettist, Lorenzo da Ponte. *Cosi* is supposed to be a telling story of human frailty and fickleness, and at its close the characters should be wiser and sadder.

Arnold Östman, the musical director of Sweden's famous Drottning-holm Court Theatre, leads a very brisk performance on period instruments, with only thirty players. The effect is crisp, clean, and unsentimental Mozart. There are no star turns here; this is the ultimate ensemble opera and is treated as such.

All the singers look their parts, and their singing is never less than good. Best are Enzo Florimo as a genuinely snide Don Alfonso and Ulla Severin as a cynical, class-conscious Despina. Not far behind is Anne-Christine Biel's duplicitous Fiordiligi. Lars Tibell sings sharp a bit too often as Ferrando, and Magnus Linden is a respectable Guglielmo. But the play's the thing here, and this is a great performance of a complicated work. Don't miss it.

■ Mozart: *Così fan tutte*

Helena Döse, Sylvia Lindenstrand, Danièle Perriers, Anson Austin, Thomas Allen, Franz Pétri, soloists; London Philharmonic Orchestra, Glyndebourne Festival Chorus, John Pritchard, cond.

VAI, color, 1975, 150 minutes. Italian with English subtitles.

The problem with *Così* has been and always will be how to play it; it's funny but not particularly lighthearted. As is the case with most Glyndebourne productions, this one is satisfying, well-sung, and beautifully played. Under Adrian Slack's direction, Glyndebourne has taken a middle ground, retaining some of the irony but not much of the bite. An intelligent, informed interpretation, it doesn't take any chances. Some listeners may be irritated by this careful approach; others will be totally satisfied with it.

The performances themselves are good. Helena Döse's Fiordiligi will not erase memories of Elisabeth Schwarzkopf, but she gets through the music admirably and cuts an elegant figure. Sylvia Lindenstrand is an all-purpose Dorabella, but she is no vocal wizard and has difficulties with parts of the score. Danièle Perriers's Despina is a bit too cute, but she sings and acts well.

The men, for the most part, fare better. Thomas Allen is an excellent Guglielmo—suave, nervous, outraged—and always tonally handsome. Anson Austin is not in the same class, but his Ferrando is a good foil to Allen's Guglielmo. And both men are rightly at a loss when up against Franz Petri's Don Alfonso. His is a fine portrayal, and one wishes he were in a less cautious production. Conductor Pritchard keeps everything moving, a bit slowly but beautifully nonetheless.

In short, this is a good, well-rounded *Così*, recommended but still taking second place to the Swedish rendering.

■ Verdi: *Don Carlo*

Luis Lima, Ileana Cotrubas, Bruna Baglioni, Giorgio Zancanaro, Robert Lloyd, Joseph Rouleau, other soloists; Royal Opera Chorus, Orchestra of the Royal Opera House, Covent Garden, Bernard Haitink, cond.

Home Vision, color, 1985, 207 minutes (two cassettes). Italian with English subtitles.

This production is uneven, but its pluses eventually outweigh its minuses. Overall, it is a thoughtful, handsome rendering of a complicated work.

Luchino Visconti's 1958 production, scenery, and costumes are a testament to quality. Christopher Renshaw's intelligent staging is helped along by Brian Large's canny direction for the small screen.

Ileana Cotrubas is a dignified, imperious Elisabetta who sings lustrously and with great attention to the nuances of the text. The close-ups of her are jarring, however, since she looks more like Don Carlo's grandmother than his young, lovely stepmother. Luis Lima is a very young-looking Carlo, and the contrast is unfortunate. Lima sings ardently but his acting is overwrought. (This may be done purposely—the historical Don Carlo *was* a bit crazy—but it's out of place here.)

Robert Lloyd's Philip II is a towering figure, pitiable and hateful at the same time, and this release is worth owning for his performance alone. Joseph Rouleau's Grand Inquisitor is nasty and snarling, and his duet with Lloyd is terrifying in its intensity—just what Verdi hoped for. Giorgio Zancanaro is a golden-toned Rodrigo, with a true Italian baritone's top and sense of legato.

All seems to be going well until Bruna Baglioni, as Eboli, appears. Both her veil song and "O don fatale" are very badly sung. Eboli is a pivotal role, and no *Don Carlo* can be a success without a fine singer in the part.

Bernard Haitink leads with sensitivity and sweep, favoring somewhat slow tempi that are a drawback only occasionally, such as in the famous "Oath" duet, where more thrust would be welcome. The orchestra plays brilliantly, but the Covent Garden chorus seems to have been having an off night. The picture quality during the first act is not as good as it should be, but it clears up soon enough. And so, if you can tolerate Baglioni and a ragged chorus, this is the version for you. Otherwise, stick to the Met's performance.

■ Verdi: *Don Carlo*

Placido Domingo, Mirella Freni, Grace Bumbry, Louis Quilico, Nicolai Ghiaurov, Ferruccio Furlanetto; Orchestra and Chorus of the Metropolitan Opera, James Levine, cond.

Paramount Home Video, color, 1983, 214 minutes (two cassettes). Italian with English subtitles.

When this performance was taped in 1983, there was hardly a better *Don Carlo* cast available in the world. Verdi's longest and possibly most complicated work requires teamwork, an opulent production, good singing actors, and a sympathetic conductor to make it work. With one or two exceptions, this version fills the bill.

The exceptions are the two basses. Ghiaurov was still an imposing, fascinating Philip II in 1983, but here he is in poor voice and much of the music sounds like a chore for him. One would be hard pressed to find specific fault with Ferruccio Furlanetto's Grand Inquisitor, but he lacks both dramatic and vocal stature in a role that requires it absolutely. The other problem is that John Dexter's production looks cheap. This is particularly disturbing in the grand auto-da-fé scene, when the awesome temporal power of the church should overwhelm the viewer.

These quibbles aside, we have much to admire here. Domingo is an ardent, sincere, and appealing Don Carlo. He has a long and somewhat thankless role but manages to convey the character's heroism, torment, and sensitivity with urgency and passion. His voice is at its freest and most ringing (this may be his finest performance on videocassette). His Elisabetta is the always vibrant Mirella Freni, here seen and heard at her loveliest, infusing the music with dignity and a well-rounded tone. Her "Tu che le vanità" is a model of how this aria should be sung. Grace Bumbry is the Eboli, back, happily, in the mezzo range, where she has always been more comfortable. Beautifully costumed and wearing a sinister eyepatch, her Eboli is arrogant until she realizes the error of her ways. She repents and we are moved. "O don fatale" is marred by some sharping above the staff, but it is an epic reading of an epic aria. Louis Quilico as Rodrigo tries so hard to articulate and make dramatic points that one appreciates his effort rather than feeling for the character he's portraying. Still, he doesn't spoil the show.

Television director Brian Large has gone for grand tableaux, which is right for this opera. James Levine's pacing of this great work is suitably stately, and he allows the drama to unfold naturally. The orchestra and chorus are in perfect accord and perform magnificently. Despite a few reservations, this production is highly recommended.

■ Mozart: *Don Giovanni*

Benjamin Luxon, Stafford Dean, Rachel Yakar, Horiana Branisteanu, Leo Goeke, Elizabeth Gale, John Rawnsley, Pierre Thau; London Philharmonic Orchestra and the Glyndebourne Chorus, Bernard Haitink, cond. Directed by Peter Hall, designed by John Bury. Directed for television by Dave Heather.

VAI, color, 1977, 173 minutes. Italian with English subtitles.

England's Glyndebourne Festival prides itself on the quality of its Mozart productions, but almost everything is wrong with this one. The blame lies largely with director Peter Hall. He decided to move the opera out of Spain and stage it in England in the Victorian period (complete with umbrellas). He also refused to allow his characters to show emotion. When Donna Elvira enters in the final banquet scene, she walks in as if she were about to borrow a cup of sugar. Where's the rage? the comedy? the pathos or caring?

Designer John Bury's drab and depressing sets not only lack color but also loom gloomily over the proceedings—and are distracting and inappropriate. The last to take blame must be the usually reliable TV director Dave Heather, who tends to play with the cameras here like a kid with a new toy. His shots of disembodied singing heads in the ensemble numbers are unfortunate.

If the individual performances were good, almost all would be forgiven, but that is not the case here. Benjamin Luxon, a fine singer, hardly cuts an elegant figure, and his voice lacks the suavity and/or menace that the Don requires. Rachel Yakar is too frequently piercing as Donna Elvira, and Horiana Branisteanu is almost invisible as Donna Anna. (The lighting is so poor that so is almost everyone else.) Leo Goeke is a sincere Ottavio, but he's often off pitch. Elizabeth Gale and John Rawnsley are excellent as Zerlina and Masetto. The rest of the cast and the orchestra and chorus are first-rate.

This tape should not be bought or rented simply because of the Glyndebourne name. Even great opera companies have an off day.

■ Strauss: *Elektra*

Birgit Nilsson, Leonie Rysanek, Mignon Dunn, Robert Nagy, Donald McIntyre, other soloists; Orchestra and Chorus of the Metropolitan Opera, James Levine, cond.

Paramount Home Video, color, 1980, 112 minutes. German with English subtitles.

Richard Strauss's one-act opera *Elektra* was first performed in Dresden in 1909. Three years before, his other one-act shocker *Salome* had startled that city, so the people of Dresden were now ready for anything. (Not so the Metropolitan Opera's audience in New York: *Salome* received only one performance in 1907 before the Met's conservative sponsors demanded that it be withdrawn.) This performance of *Elektra* was given in February 1980, and it was only the fifty-eighth time the Met had staged the work. Someone is to be thanked that it was telecast. The only question is, what took them so long to release it?

Birgit Nilsson was a powerhouse of a singer, even at this point in her career (she was sixty-one years old). Her tone, when focused, has a laser-like effect, although there is a bit of straying from pitch early on. But for the most part, she soars through the music like a woman possessed (which is just what Elektra is), and her acting is surprisingly good. She is a great listener (the intelligent camerawork helps here) in her confrontations with Chrysothemis and Klytemnestra, and the hate she conveys as she sends Aegisth to his death is palpable. Her final dance of triumph is less a dance than a lurch, but it is effective nonetheless. This is a portrayal for the ages.

The rest of the cast is no less good. Rysanek, as Chrysothemis, had everything: the voice is all of a piece, the top is cutting and pointed, the interpretation riveting. Mignon Dunn is a fine (if slightly too robust) Klytemnestra; her maniacal laughter at her exit is as memorable and spine-chilling as her death shriek. Donald McIntyre is a regal Orest, and Robert Nagy a suitably loathsome Aegisth. The rest of the singers are fine. Conductor Levine gets wonderful, if extremely loud, playing out of the Met forces most of the time. (He almost drowns Nilsson out.) Nonetheless, he manages to turn tender during the recognition scene.

The sets and costumes by Rudolf Heinrich are nondescript, but TV director Brian Large spares us by relying heavily on close-ups of the principals. At times, the camera has trouble finding the correct focus, but this is a minor problem. Few of Nilsson's performances are available on videocassette, and *Elektra* was a crowning achievement of her long career. This is a great performance of a great opera, and a must for any serious collector.

■ Mozart: *Die Entführung aus dem Serail*

Valerie Masterson, Lillian Watson, Ryland Davies, James Hoback, Willard White; London Philharmonic Orchestra and Glyndebourne Festival Chorus, Gustav Kuhn, cond.

VAI, color, 1980, 145 minutes. German with English subtitles.

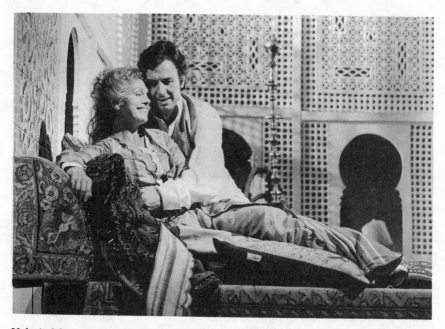

Valerie Masterson and Ryland Davies in a scene from the Glyndebourne Festival production of Mozart's *Die Entführung aus dem Serail*. Courtesy Video Artists International.

William Dudley's sets, all in pastels with elaborate grillwork and featuring live doves in a huge cage, add to the charm of this souvenir of the 1980 Glyndebourne Festival. Mozart's lovely singspiel comes to life under Peter Wood's direction as well, and the singing is consistently high-level.

Ryland Davies uses his honey-toned tenor to fine advantage as Belmonte, singing the difficult "Ich baue ganz" with grace and ease. Valerie Masterson looks and sounds radiant as his beloved Constanze, turning in a meltingly lyrical "Traurigkeit" and an exciting, if not quite technically flawless, "Martern aller Arten." Lillian Watson and James Hoback as the second couple, Blonde and Pedrillo, are lively and convincing. Bass Willard White makes Osmin truly menacing instead of a mere buffoon, and he sings with great richness and expressivity. In the speaking role of Pasha Selim, Joachim Bissmeier is, by turns, threatening and forgiving.

The sound is not quite up to par: the bass is too resonant and the treble tends to distort. Played at low volume, however, it shouldn't offend, and the production itself is not to be missed.

■ Verdi: *Ernani*

Placido Domingo, Mirella Freni, Renato Bruson, Nicolai Ghiaurov; Orchestra and Chorus of La Scala, Milan, Riccardo Muti, cond.

HBO Video, color, 1982, 135 minutes. Italian with English subtitles.

Ernani has enough melodies to fill three operas, and if we cannot get involved with the plot because it hinges on an antiquated code of honor, we can identify with the characters on a scene-by-scene basis. But if neither the melodic invention nor the situational drama works for you, the sheer thrill of hearing the human voice in glorious action definitely should do the trick.

The problems with this production are nonvocal and stem from the idea, apparently shared by director Luca Ronconi and designer Ezio Frigerio, that *Ernani* is unstageworthy and dramatically dull. How else can we interpret the many ways they found to sabotage the production? Frigerio, for instance, has created a six-foot pit in the middle of the stage for the chorus, in which it resembles nothing so much as a set of singing torsos. Equally puzzling, Ronconi has invited on stage a bloc of extras garbed in evening clothes. The singers are left to do pretty much whatever strikes their fancy. Much to their credit, they don't make fools of themselves.

But *Ernani* is valued for its singing and orchestral work, and here we get almost enough of the great kind. Muti infuses the work with youthful energy and authority, though it takes the cast about one act to warm up, presumably because they are afraid of falling into the Black Hole on the stage. Domingo, in the title role, is superb, singing with big tone and robust involvement. Don Carlo, the baritone, has the most mature and interesting music, and Bruson is as smooth as silk, sensitive to the text, and in handsome, burnished voice. Ghiaurov sounds a bit too old as Silva. All of the assisting singers are first-rate.

Has any soprano, with the exception of Rosa Ponselle, ever sung Elvira's "Ernani! involami," and the cabaletta that follows, as it should be sung? The role itself is elusive: although it has lots of stirring music,

Nicolai Ghiaurov and Placido Domingo in the La Scala production of Verdi's *Ernani*. Photo by Lelli & Masotti. Courtesy HBO Video.

plenty of high notes, much good ensemble work, and more than enough individual moments of angst, it's difficult to tell what the character of Elvira is all about. Mirella Freni, however, is lovely. Her basically lyric soprano has mellowed and aged and now carries prestige and authority. She makes excellent dramatic points throughout and, after a shaky opening scene, sings gloriously.

In summation: a ludicrous production, but a great tenor and baritone, a bass at less than his best, a fine conductor, and a great soprano. Worth having.

■ Verdi: *Ernani*

Luciano Pavarotti, Leona Mitchell, Sherrill Milnes, Ruggero Raimondi; Orchestra and Chorus of the Metropolitan Opera, James Levine, cond.

Paramount Home Video, color, 1983, 142 minutes. Italian with English subtitles.

Verdi's fifth opera, *Ernani*, has always been on the verge of becoming a repertory staple. Its failure to make it might be attributed by some people to the gimmick in the plot—the hero commits suicide out of a peculiarly misplaced sense of honor, and modern audiences may find his motive less than convincing. The opera also requires four strong Verdi singers, and they've become more and more difficult to find in recent years. But *Ernani* does have beautiful music for the soloists, many stirring choruses, and several well-wrought ensembles.

One problem with this particular production is the production itself. The settings and direction are by Pier Luigi Samaritani, who has designed a vista of such CinemaScopic proportions that the characters are lost in it. There are drapes, staircases, enormous potted palms, much chiffon, and lots of handsome and conventional furniture. The singers stand and deliver—hand to heart, hand to forehead—making it impossible for us to get emotionally involved with this production at all.

Nevertheless, Levine plays the work for its lyricism and gives his singers plenty of room. Pavarotti is given more to do than most Ernanis (this production includes an extraordinary aria and cabaletta that Verdi composed for the Russian tenor Nicola Ivanoff in 1844), and he is in glorious, ringing voice. Don Carlo, the baritone, has the most mature music in the opera, and Sherrill Milnes is impressive, singing right on the note, with manliness and regality. Silva is not the most fascinating of parts, and Ruggero Raimondi, sounding a bit hoarse, makes little of it. The rest of the cast is fine.

The heroine, Elvira, is a long and difficult role, with dramatic outbursts and hard-to-define emotions. Leona Mitchell delivers an astonishingly mediocre performance for a major singer. Indeed, she sinks the Met's ship in this production. She sings all the notes, weak bottom ones notwithstanding (phrases that lie low are barely completed), but seems devoid of temperament. In addition, her voice simply does not have the right timbre for the role, and she breathes in unmusical places, breaking phrases and robbing them of their effect.

In summary: a murky production, a great tenor and baritone, a bass somewhat off form, a fine conductor, and a totally miscast soprano. The La Scala performance on HBO Video is also uninteresting visually but much better to listen to.

■ Tchaikovsky: *Eugene Onegin*

Mirella Freni, Sandra Walker, Peter Dvorsky, Wolfgang Brendel, Nicolai Ghiaurov; Orchestra and Chorus of the Lyric Opera of Chicago, the Chicago City Ballet, Bruno Bartoletti, cond.

Home Vision, color, 1985, 157 minutes (two cassettes). Russian with English subtitles.

Eugene Onegin is considered by many to be Tchaikovsky's masterpiece. This tale of cynicism, innocence, and maturation presents philosophical and psychological questions normally ignored in most popular operas. The music always suits its subject, while maintaining a melodic lushness that only the late romantics could conjure up. This particular production is splendid.

This performance features Mirella Freni's first Tatiana and it is a great success. Impetuous and girlish in the first act, with an impassioned letter scene, Freni grows emotionally over the course of the opera, and her heartbreak and eventual spurning of Onegin seem to come naturally from within. Moreover, Freni sounds as fresh as she did a decade ago. Sandra Walker, as Olga, offers good vocal support but appears uncomfortable in the role.

Peter Dvorsky is a fine tenor, and his Lensky is quite believable. He deserves the ovation he receives after his great aria. Ghiaurov sings his familiar Gremin, a bit dryer than in years gone by, but still a wise and interesting figure. In the title role, Wolfgang Brendel is impressive as an unsympathetic character in the first two acts, winning us over in his final duet with Freni, in which he uses his bright baritone with passion and intelligence.

The remainder of the cast, including the ballet corps, deserves great praise, and conductor Bartoletti holds the opera's folksy and elegant elements together with knowledge and understanding. Pier Luigi Samaritani's sets, costumes, and direction are greatly helped by Kirk Browning's TV direction, which works particularly well in the second act duel scene.

The only drawback to this generally excellent production is the somewhat cloudy picture and the distortion of the sound above a certain level. (These may have been problems with the review copy, but they're worth checking out before investing.) Otherwise, *bravi!*

■ Verdi: *Falstaff*

Renato Bruson, Katia Ricciarelli, Barbara Hendricks, Brenda Boozer, Lucia Valentini Terrani, Dalmacio Gonzalez, Leo Nucci; Orchestra and Chorus of the Royal Opera House, Covent Gardent, Carlo Maria Giulini, cond.

HBO Video, 1983, color, 141 minutes. Italian with English subtitles.

Falstaff, Verdi's witty, life-affirming opera, is a masterpiece of his last years. Most opera companies do not attempt to produce this intricate work unless they are going to try to do it as well as possible. Such is the case with this performance, which is hampered only by Hayden Griffith and Michael Stennett's airless and cluttered production. TV director Brian Large helps out stage director Ronald Eyre whenever he can by placing his cameras in telling, dramatically apt positions—he "opens up" the production by homing in on the details. The difficult second-act ensemble is a case in point: the camerawork helps to make the scene crystal-clear.

Renato Bruson, in the title role, refuses to vulgarize and portrays Falstaff as a wonderfully human fool. His Falstaff is also aware that he is a knight—he doesn't wiggle or sing falsetto—and his "Quand'ero paggio" is so delicately and beautifully sung that we can imagine the lithe, young Falstaff of the past and almost understand his gross vanity. His sound is always handsome, his demeanor full of grace. It's a wonderful impersonation.

Katia Ricciarelli is in good voice, although she is less perky and droll than the ideal Mistress Ford; there is little jolliness in her reading. But Brenda Boozer as Meg and Lucia Valentini Terrani as Mistress Quickly move with robust joy and sing with great energy. Barbara Hendricks and Dalmacio Gonzales as Nannetta and Fenton are exemplary, but special praise goes to Hendricks for her voice of pure silver. Leo Nucci is more than up to the vocal demands of Ford, but his broad acting is out of keeping with the rest of the cast. The smaller roles are all well taken.

Falstaff has always been known as a conductor's opera, and it's clearly Giulini's show. Aware that Verdi's orchestral arrangements strongly underscore the meaning of the singers' words, he doesn't miss a chance to get a smile from the orchestra. His generally slow tempi tend, oddly, to suppress the rambunctiousness that this opera requires, but his is a valid view of the work and the score is lovingly and knowingly rendered. This is grand Verdi, performed in a grand manner.

Leo Nucci and Renato Bruson in a scene from the Royal Opera production of Verdi's *Falstaff*. Photo by Zoë Dominic. Courtesy HBO Video.

■ Verdi: *Falstaff*

Donald Gramm, Kay Griffel, Reni Penkova, Elizabeth Gale, Nucci Condo, Max-René Cosotti, Benjamin Luxon; London Philharmonic Orchestra, Glyndebourne Chorus, John Pritchard, cond.

VAI, color, 1976, 123 minutes. Italian with English subtitles.

Glyndebourne has succeeded magnificently with this *Falstaff*, one of its finest efforts. The late Jean-Pierre Ponnelle offers us an airy and light production, perfectly suited to the ebullience of this work. The gifted Dave Heather has directed effectively for the small screen as well, and from a visual standpoint this whole undertaking has been well thought out.

Vocally, there are few complaints. Donald Gramm is a superb Falstaff,

Donald Gramm as Sir John Falstaff in the Glyndebourne Festival production of Verdi's *Falstaff*. Courtesy Video Artists International.

finely drawn, full of false arrogance, and totally lacking in self-awareness. Seeing him in his second-act finery is a delight. As for the rest of the cast, there are no star turns, seemingly by design. Conductor John Pritchard emphasizes the ensemble, not the individual, and plays the comedy for its quicksilver qualities, with appropriate tempi. (His reading of the score takes a quarter hour less than Giulini's.) The entire cast is praiseworthy, but Benjamin Luxon's Ford is truly magnificent and his big second-act aria is a mini-opera in itself. The final fugue, performed in front of the curtain, is so joyful that we are ready to see the whole performance over again.

There is no clear choice between this and HBO Video's tape; Pritchard is funnier and lighter, and Giulini is warmer and more charming. We are presented with an embarrassment of riches in *Falstaff*, one of the greatest operas ever written.

■ Beethoven: *Fidelio*

Elisabeth Söderström, Anton de Ridder, Elizabeth Gale, Ian Caley, Curt Appelgren, Robert Allman, Michael Langdon; the London Philharmonic Orchestra and Glyndebourne Festival Chorus, Bernard Haitink, cond.

VAI, color, 1979, 130 minutes. German with English subtitles.

Beethoven's only opera holds great fascination, and each new production inspires new debate. Its peculiar construction, with the first act in the singspiel tradition and the second in the more familiar dramatic operatic form, always poses problems. TV director Dave Heather doesn't solve any of them in this performance. He relies too heavily on close-ups and has the singers strike poses and sing directly into the camera instead of to each other, which spoils the dramatic effect and lessens the emotional impact.

What detracts seriously from the production is the Florestan of Anton de Ridder, whose tenor is unsuited to, and almost defeated by, Beethoven's difficult vocal line. Furthermore, Robert Allman's Pizarro is weak, and Michael Langdon is almost near the end of his vocal tether as Don Fernando. Ian Caley is a nice, if unidiomatic Jacquino, and Elizabeth Gale is a perky, lovely Marzelline. Curt Appelgren is warm and understanding as Rocco.

The crucial element here is the Leonore of the superb Swedish soprano Elisabeth Söderström, who perfectly captures Leonore's radiance, goodness, and outrage and sings with security and passion. Hers is an irreplaceable interpretation.

Bernard Haitink, the LPO, and the Glyndebourne Chorus are so good that one almost forgets the minuses in this performance. The overall effect is of a successful undertaking, but be warned—there are serious performance flaws throughout.

Elisabeth Söderström as Leonore in the Glyndebourne Festival production of Beethoven's *Fidelio*. Courtesy Video Artists International.

■ Strauss: *Die Fledermaus*

Joan Sutherland, Monique Brynnel, Anson Austin, Robert Gard, Michael Lewis, Heather Begg; the Australian Opera Chorus, the Elizabethan Sydney Orchestra, Richard Bonynge, cond. Directed by Anthony Besch; designed by John Stoddart.

Sony, color, 1982, 142 minutes. English.

The only reason for owning this English-language *Fledermaus* is the presence of Joan Sutherland, although many of her admirers will be disappointed by her performance. She acts the role of Rosalinda as a dowager empress and sings with a heavy tone unsuited to the part. Her sense of comedy is good but comes close to real brilliance only in the second-act dialogue when she is disguised as a Hungarian countess. It doesn't matter that she embellishes the vocal line—that's what we expect—but her interpretation is not a success.

Monique Brynnel is a spirited Adele but has a sharp edge to the top of her voice—and an inappropriate Swedish accent as well. She sounds more like a lyric soprano than a coloratura and can't handle some of the more florid music. Robert Gard is a tenor Eisenstein and, though he sings impressively, he acts stiffly and unconvincingly. Anson Austin, as Alfred, speaks throughout with a distracting Italian accent and never takes his eyes off the conductor, which tends to lessen the drama. Heather Begg is not the usual caricature of Orlofsky, but her voice is unimpressive; and Michael Lewis's Falke is sturdy but dull. The audience laughs only three or four times during the first two acts (a bad sign), and the humor in the third act is embarrassingly broad.

The sets and costumes are beautiful but can't save this performance. When Richard Bonynge's lackluster conducting does take flight, the music sounds like a Gilbert and Sullivan operetta. The party scene has the added doubtful attraction of the pas de deux from *Don Quixote* uninspiredly danced by Lois Strike and Kelvin Coe.

This *Fledermaus* is a decidedly provincial and heavy-footed affair—even the first-act trio is a dud. It does everyone—particularly Johann Strauss—a disservice.

■ Zandonai: *Francesca da Rimini*

Renata Scotto, Placido Domingo, Cornell MacNeil, William Lewis, Isola Jones, Richard Fredericks; Chorus and Orchestra of the Metropolitan Opera, James Levine, cond.

Paramount Home Video, color, 1984, 148 minutes. Italian with English subtitles.

Who would have believed that Zandonai's overly fragrant period piece of 1914 would receive such an exquisite production at the Met—or anywhere else, for that matter? Though hardly a masterpiece, the work contains a lovely duet or two and is so unashamed of its excesses that it's impossible to dislike it entirely. The first act contains the most anxiously awaited entrance for the lead tenor in operatic history, and to add mystery to anxiety, he doesn't sing a note when he does arrive. There are also ten-minute stretches that are noisy and clamorous but other periods of such rapture that they seem to come from another opera entirely. The Met's show, designed by Ezio Frigerio (with costumes by Franca Squarciapino that must be seen to be believed), is perfectly in keeping with the opera's pre-Raphaelite conception. Piero Faggioni's directing is ideal.

TV director Brian Large also does an excellent job, taking us from scene to scene, pointing out the loveliest, most dramatic, most flowery moments. Fortunately, his pair of adulterous young lovers are worth focusing on.

Renata Scotto was still singing well in 1984, although when she sings both loud and high the sound is truly awful. Her part of the third-act duet does not lie very high, so she is at her best here. Dramatically, Scotto has always seen herself as bigger than she actually is—with a bigger voice, to boot—so her grand gestures in this performance are right on target. She is more than ably partnered by Domingo, here heard and seen at his most persuasive. His voice rings true and clear, and he acts with passion and dignity. For a tenor who has never been known as a high-note expert, he seems to have no fear of the role's stratospheric tessitura.

Cornell MacNeil sings the role of the villainous Gianciotto with gigantic volume and no subtlety, which is just what it requires. William Lewis is suitably loathsome as the one-eyed Malatestino. Isola Jones plays the handmaiden Smaragdi sympathetically, and Richard Fredricks is impressive as Francesca's brother. The remainder of the large cast is excellent. James Levine lingers lovingly over the many romantic moments, with particular attention to the smoldering third-act duet, which climaxes in the lovers' kiss. Everything takes slightly too long in this opera—but that's Zandonai's fault, not Levine's.

If you like your opera well wrought and a bit perfumed, this performance will please you. Even if you don't, try it anyway. It could just cure the blues.

■ Weber: *Der Freischütz*

Catarina Ligendza, Toni Kramer, Raili Viljakainen, Wolfgang Schoene, Wolfgang Probst, others; Chorus and Orchestra of the Württemberg State Opera, Stuttgart, Dennis Russell Davies, cond. Designed and directed by Achim Freyer.

Home Vision, color, 1981, 150 minutes. German with English subtitles.

Der Freischütz is considered the first romantic German opera. It's difficult to mount successfully: its combination of folksiness and the supernatural, together with the use of spoken dialogue interspersed with music, can add up to a director's nightmare. In this case the interesting and occasionally revolutionary Achim Freyer has designed a surreal set, with doors set into painted landscape into and out of which the characters mysteriously keep wandering. There are other inscrutable elements. What do the rainbow and all-seeing eye signify? Why do the lively bridesmaids' and huntsmen's choruses seem to be parodies of the text? Are we supposed to laugh, become enraged, or take it all as a piece of German decadence? Freyer himself never makes it clear, and there's not a clue in Home Vision's booklet about the production.

Max is sung by the young heldentenor Toni Kramer, who is less impressive here than his present reputation would lead us to expect. Catarina Ligendza does not have the loveliest of tones, but she is quite thrilling and even moving. Wolfgang Probst sings Caspar's music with an apt sneer and is very effective, indeed. Finnish soprano Raili Viljakainen is a fine Ännchen, and the rest of the cast is quite good.

The production is odd, but the wolf's glen scene is admirably frightening, and the lighting by Hans Joachim-Haas transforms the work into a sort of bad dream. Conductor Dennis Russell Davies's taut reading emphasizes the score's underlying tension, and the chorus performs with fervor. The orchestra of the Württemberg State Opera gives a first-rate performance, steeped as it is in the work's background and tradition.

Der Freischütz has often been criticized as static, but this production catches fire and makes an impression. It's recommended not only for those who have never seen the opera but also for those who know it well and want to see another interpretation.

■ Britten: *Gloriana*

Sarah Walker, Anthony Rolfe Johnson, Richard van Allan, Alan Opie, Elizabeth Vaughan, other soloists; Orchestra and Chorus of the English National Opera, Mark Elder, cond.

HBO Video, color, 1984, 146 minutes. English.

None of Benjamin Britten's operas is easy, either melodically or textually, but *Gloriana* is particularly difficult. Composed for the coronation of Queen Elizabeth II in 1953, it presents a relatively bleak picture of the queen's Tudor namesake. "I see no weighty reason that I should be fond to live or fear to die," Gloriana's last words, drew much ire from the British public, which frowned on these coronation sentiments. Nevertheless, the libretto by William Plomer is as rich as Britten's score, and both seem to have become better with time. This performance dates from 1984 at the English National Opera, and it is an intense, worthwhile experience. Elizabeth and Essex have been treated operatically before (Donizetti's *Roberto Devereux* comes immediately to mind), but never with such emotional and historical acumen.

As the Virgin Queen, Sarah Walker fairly overwhelms. Towering over everyone, as she should, she is every inch the monarch, and her diction and singing are superb. Anthony Rolfe Johnson is a wonderfully complicated Essex, Alan Opie a strong Cecil, and Richard van Allan sings and acts a politically suave Sir Walter Raleigh. Elizabeth Vaughan as the arrogant Lady Rich is also a great asset.

The sets and costumes are properly lavish, and Colin Graham's direction (assisted for the small screen by Derek Bailey) never falters, always adding to our understanding of the drama. The orchestra plays the rich score with verve and precision, and conductor Elder manages to make the music seem both brand-new and accessible. This is a thorny Tudor rose in some ways—but definitely worth picking.

■ Humperdinck: *Hansel and Gretel*

Judith Blegen, Frederica von Stade, Jean Kraft, Michael Devlin, Diane Kesling, Betsy Norden, Rosalind Elias; Orchestra, Chorus and Ballet of the Metropolitan Opera, Thomas Fulton, cond. Directed by Nathaniel Merrill; designed by Robert O'Hearn.

Paramount Home Video, color, 1982, 104 minutes. English.

This is a great opera, even if it is sometimes looked on as a musical bonbon for the kiddies. The score's Wagnerian orchestration, exquisite melodies, and textural niceties are all too frequently overlooked. The VCR now enables youngsters and their parents to view the opera's special moments. This imaginative Met production is worth seeing again and again, especially as it is presented in easily understood English.

Everyone involved in this taping is to be commended. Blegen as Gretel and von Stade as Hansel are an ideal sister-and-brother act; they jump around like real children, sound wonderful, and enunciate clearly. Kraft and Devlin, as their parents, are by turns angry, worried, repentant, and overjoyed. Betsy Norden's Dew Fairy is lovely, and Diane Kesling's Sandman is handsomely sung.

But, by dint of grotesque makeup and the role itself, kudos go to Rosalind Elias as the green-tongued Witch. She cavorts and menaces quite convincingly and sings her difficult music well. And that broomstick! Congratulations, too, to the production team and to TV director Kirk Browning. *Bravi!*

■ Strauss: *Intermezzo*

Felicity Lott, John Pringle, Ian Caley; London Philharmonic Orchestra, Gustav Kuhn, cond. A Glyndebourne Festival production. Directed by John Cox; designed by Martin Battersby. English translation by Andrew Porter.

Home Vision, color, 1983, 155 minutes. English.

It was no secret that Strauss's wife, Pauline, was given to embarrassing remarks about him and his music. Her social gaffes and relentless hectoring have even been blamed for the decline in Strauss's musical enterprise later in life. In 1923, however, he was still at the height of his powers. Having recently triumphed with *Die Frau ohne Schatten*, he was ready to try something less Wagnerian and more along the lines of Offenbach: domestic intrigues, harmless flirtations, light and effervescent music. He succeeded magnificently with *Intermezzo*. The work is conversational—almost more like a play than an opera—but for Strauss aficionados, it is highly effective both as opera and as drama.

The opera was conceived as early as 1916, and Strauss worked on the score in his spare time. Hugo von Hofmannsthal, his great collaborator at the time, liked the idea of doing a delicate comedy but loathed Strauss's Offenbachish approach and advised Strauss to work with the dramatist Hermann Bahr. But Strauss and Bahr could not agree, and so Strauss finally completed the libretto himself. He finished the score on August 21, 1923, and the work was premiered in Dresden on November 4, 1924. After the premiere, soprano Lotte Lehmann, who created the role of Christine, complimented Pauline Strauss on the lovely gift her husband had created for her with this opera. "I don't give a damn," Pauline replied. Onlookers were shocked, but Strauss reportedly smiled indulgently.

Glyndebourne is an ideal environment for this intimate and personal work. The character of Christine is a thinly disguised Frau Strauss, and she turns out, despite her mood swings, to be rather appealing as portrayed by Felicity Lott. Hers is a genuine Strauss voice, basically lyric but endowed with a large and blooming top register. She is admirably partnered by John Pringle as her husband and by Ian Caley as the penniless young baron with whom she has an innocent fling. Gustav Kuhn's musical leadership makes one wonder why *Intermezzo* isn't heard more often.

TV director David Buckton uses his cameras sensitively to catch the nuances of John Cox's uncluttered staging and the sensuous hues of the art nouveau decor designed by Martin Battersby. This is a fine rendering of a specialist's opera—perhaps it will even help to popularize it.

■ Wagner: *Lohengrin*

Peter Hofmann, Eva Marton, Leonie Rysanek, Leif Roar; Metropolitan Opera Orchestra and Chorus, James Levine, cond. Directed by August Everding; designed by Ming Cho Lee.

Paramount Home Video, color, 1986, 220 minutes. German with English subtitles.

Lohengrin was the turning point in Richard Wagner's career. Completed in 1848, it was his last opera in the prevailing Romantic German style best typified by Weber. He radically altered his musical language in the next four works, which constitute the *Ring* cycle, and in the later operas. In so doing, he also reshaped the course of musical history and the lyric theatre. While *Lohengrin* may sound old-fashioned from the vantage point of *Tristan und Isolde*, it contains harmonic textures that presage *Parsifal*, the composer's final work.

Interestingly, this production by the Metropolitan Opera was originally staged in 1976 and reflects some of the transitional aspects of stage production and mise-en-scène in this century. Ming Cho Lee's sets are neither fully realistic nor entirely abstract, but they are attractive and work effectively on the small screen. Lohengrin emerges from a riverbank, but the swan that draws him up the Rhine is merely a brilliant white light beaming up from the rear scrim. Otherwise, August Everding's neonaturalistic approach is clear and practical, making excellent use of the Met's technical resources to convey the work's symbolic and spectacular aspects.

The cast is about as good as can be expected in an age when singers with voices big enough to cut through large orchestrations are increasingly rare. Peter Hofmann looks and acts the part of the swan knight, but his voice tends to wobble under stress, which is much of the time. Sopranos who sing the role of Elsa generally fall into two categories: those who convey the girlish qualities but lack the vocal weight to dominate the big ensembles and high dramatic passages, and those with big voices who lack the delicacy that the role demands. For the most part, Eva Marton bridges this gap. She has a large enough instrument to ride the big ensembles and full orchestration, especially at the close of the first act. She also has the sweetness to convey the emotions of the heroine in her entrance aria, "Enisam in trüben Tagen." She is a believable, touching Elsa.

Leif Roar has the more difficult role, for he must make the weak Telramund more than a whining, henpecked spouse, and he succeeds admirably. Leonie Rysanek as the evil Ortrud (she was a notable Elsa in the 1950s) steals the show in this new role, which she recently began undertaking. Hers is by far the most compelling and energetic performance among a relatively strong cast, both vocally and histrionically.

James Levine's approach to the score is leisurely but not tedious, lyrical but fully responsive to the work's big moments. He is generous to his singers, rarely pushing the orchestra to levels of sound that might tax them unnecessarily, and the orchestra responds well to his leadership. TV director Brian Large catches the full scope of the production's epic and intimate values. In all, this is a successful undertaking of a difficult work and is highly recommended.

■ Verdi: *I Lombardi*

Ghena Dimitrova, José Carreras, Silvano Carroli, Carlo Bini, soloists; Chorus and Orchestra of La Scala, Milan, Gianandrea Gavazzeni, cond.

HBO Video, color, 1984, 126 minutes. Italian with English subtitles.

Although not one of Verdi's great works, *I Lombardi* contains some stirring and beautiful music, with particularly interesting ensembles. This performance does little to make dramatic sense of the opera, and for the most part, the singers don't help. Ghena Dimitrova, as Giselda, is the lone exception. She sings passionately and with attention to the words, but her voice is not quite right for this part, and though her sound works for the larger moments, the role needs a more intimate approach. Still, she gives a generally intense and exciting reading.

Not so the normally involved José Carreras, who sounds a bit strained and, though as handsome as ever, seems unable to come to dramatic grips with the role of Oronte. (In truth, there may not be much to grasp.) Silvano Carroli sings the villainous hermit Pagano, and while he uses his baritone well, he lacks the vocal heft to bring this character to life. Carlo Bini, in the second tenor part, sings alternately flat and sharp—a feat in itself.

The sets are sparse—mostly backdrops and banners—but the cos-

Ghena Dimitrova and José Carreras in a scene from the La Scala production of Verdi's *I Lombardi*. Photo by Lelli & Masotti. Courtesy HBO Video.

tumes, all in reds, whites, and golds, are spectacular. Conductor Gian-andrea Gavazzeni leads the La Scala forces with verve and attention to detail, and the orchestra and chorus rightly garner most of the evening's applause. In all likelihood there won't be another *Lombardi* on videocassette for a long time, so if you must have one, this is it. But it's something of a disappointment.

■ Prokofiev: *The Love of Three Oranges*

Ryland Davies, Ugo Benelli, Nucci Condo, Richard van Allan, Willard White, Nelly Morpurgo, other soloists; the London Philharmonic Orchestra and Glyndebourne Festival Chorus, Bernard Haitink, cond. Designed by Maurice Sendak, directed by Frank Corsaro.

Home Vision, color, 1982, 120 minutes. French with English subtitles.

Premiered in Chicago in 1921, this work has garnered (quite inexplicably to some) a great deal of popularity and praise. The famous march from the second act is the only recognizable piece, the work is a farce, and the music is farcical as well. The plot, which concerns a king of a mythical kingdom who attempts to cure his son of hypochondria and melancholia, is based on a 1761 play by Gozzi. This Glyndebourne production is so good, with all the disparate elements pulled together, that it almost makes a case for the opera. Almost.

Sendak perfectly captures the opera's deranged zaniness in his wonderful sets and costumes, with bright colors, outlandish designs, and a gigantic puppet representing the cook from whom the three oranges are stolen. Director Frank Corsaro keeps things moving fast, and there are almost always dozens of characters onstage, each doing his or her comedy routine.

The singing and orchestral playing are excellent. Ryland Davies is a properly morose Prince, Willard White a suitably upset King, and the Fata Morgana of Nelly Morpurgo is bewitchingly sung and acted. The rest of the cast seems to take their roles seriously—as if they were performing something other than a mere musical diversion.

This tape is recommended only because it's as fine a version of this opera as we're bound to get: it's a great performance of a mysteriously popular trifle.

■ **Donizetti:** *Lucia di Lammermoor*

Joan Sutherland, Alfredo Kraus, Pablo Elvira, Paul Plishka, other soloists; Orchestra and Chorus of the Metropolitan Opera, Richard Bonynge, cond.

Paramount Home Video, color, 1982, 128 minutes. Italian with English subtitles.

This is not only a thrilling performance but also a historical one. Joan Sutherland, in her mid-fifties when this was taped, is probably one of the five or so greatest Lucias of all time, and we are lucky to have this tape to study and appreciate.

Of course, her usual flaws are present as well: mushy diction, generalized acting, scooping into notes. But the overall effect is extraordinary; this is what true bel canto is all about. Her first act is sung limpidly and with pinpoint accuracy and golden tone; her second act is full of power and thrust; and her mad scene is dazzling (taken down a semitone—the only discernible bow to her age), with rapid, accurate coloratura and passage work and real attention to the text. Though her performance may lack the dramatic insight of Sills or Callas, it's magnificent nonetheless.

Alfredo Kraus, the same age as his costar, is still a model of ease and grace, with no fear of vocal heights, although the tone is now a bit dryer. He can still create a furor when he wants to, such as when he takes a high D-flat with Sutherland at the sextet's close. No less fine is baritone Pablo Elvira, whose bright sound and snarling reading add excitement to the show. Paul Plishka's Raimondo is credible and sonorous.

The sets are adequate and the action keeps moving, if without much subtlety. Richard Bonynge seems to be following his leading lady, but it really doesn't matter. This production may be short on real drama, but it's very long on real singing.

■ **Donizetti:** *Lucia di Lammermoor*

Anna Moffo, Lajos Kozma, Guilio Fioravanti, Paolo Washington; other soloists; the RAI Chorus and Rome Symphony Orchestra, Carlo Felice Cillario, cond.

VAI, color, 1971, 108 minutes. Italian with English subtitles.

It must be said at the outset that this tape (and apparently all copies of it) is slightly fast, which renders everything close to a semitone sharp, and some people may be put off by it. In any case, it is difficult to recommend the production: too many elements in the performance are poor.

But it does have one major plus, Anna Moffo's reading of the title role. She's in wonderful, sensual voice, despite some crooning, and builds a convincing portrait. The famous mad scene comes from within her and it is beautifully sung; the close-up camera work emphasizes the character's beauty, sensitivity, and vulnerability.

The Edgardo is Lajos Kozma, an unexciting but useful tenor who looks fine but sounds pinched (the extra squeeze of the pitch doesn't help him). Giulio Fioravanti sings a dramatically effective Enrico, even if he does evoke a moustache-twirling villain of the gaslight era. Paolo Washington makes much of Raimondo, to little avail.

■ Verdi: *Macbeth*

Renato Bruson, Mara Zampieri, James Morris, Dennis O'Neill, others; Chorus and Orchestra of the Deutsche Oper, Berlin, Giuseppe Sinopoli, cond. Directed by Luca Ronconi; directed for television by Brian Large.

Home Vision, color, 1987, 150 minutes. Italian with English subtitles.

Luca Ronconi's *Macbeth* is an interesting if odd production. He seems to have more respect for this work than he did for *Ernani* (available on HBO Video), but he still has some strange ideas. Macbeth and Banquo don't walk onto the witches' scene; they rise up from a trapdoor. There is no procession for the soon-to-be-dead King Duncan; he just enters, sits down, and is admired by Macbeth and his lady. And, at the close of the apparition scene in the third act, the mists clear (i.e., the lights come up) and Lady Macbeth is seen sitting calmly at a dining room table. The sight raises the disturbing question, has Macbeth been hallucinating the whole thing while lounging comfortably in the castle?

The stage is mostly bare, the characters invariably wear red, the witches are very well dressed and well behaved, with mountains of dark hair, and most of the action takes place against a black backdrop. Brian Large has directed for TV effectively, with plenty of close-ups and a properly spooky third act, including that strange finale.

Conductor Giuseppe Sinopoli—he of the controversial tempi and dynamics—is going for a star turn here. There are an excessive number of shots of him conducting (with a white sheet behind him so that he will stand out more clearly), but he is still erratic and at times eccentric to the point of artificiality. The witches sing with real emphasis on the words, and the orchestra is in great form; but Lady Macbeth's "La luce langue" lacks orchestral and vocal atmosphere, and the banquet scene slows down bizarrely for the brindisi, making it seem like a dirge rather than a toast. The fourth-act chorus is so slow that it threatens to come to a halt entirely. It is impossible to tell what Sinopoli has in mind, other than to be controversial.

Renato Bruson's Macbeth is a fine figure of corruption and fear, although his sound is a bit gruff and the bloom is clearly off the voice. Still, it's a thoughtful, valid reading of a complex role. Mara Zampieri's hard and vibrato-free tone never varies in color from top to bottom. When she does sing softly she sounds remote and covered, and the very bottom of her voice sounds a bit like a mediocre baritone. Her strange facial expressions, which might have worked well on stage, detract from her performance on television. Though she has all the notes perfectly in place for the part (except the infamous high D-flat at the close of the sleepwalking scene, which she skips), she fails to move the viewer.

James Morris is a sonorous, brooding Banquo (it was a nice touch of Ronconi's to make him uncomfortable and suspicious from the start), and Dennis O'Neill is a sincere and secure Macduff. The rest of the cast is first-rate. The lighting, by Kurt Oskar Herting, makes the almost bare stage seem right, and gives the opera atmosphere.

Though this production can't be dismissed, a great deal of it is too quirky and gets in the way of the music. If you can own only one *Macbeth* on videocassette, stick with VAI's from Glyndebourne. It's a fascinating performance.

■ Verdi: *Macbeth*

Kostas Paskalis, Josephine Barstow, James Morris, Keith Erwen, other soloists; London Philharmonic Orchestra and Glyndebourne Chorus, John Pritchard, cond.

VAI, color, 1972, 148 minutes (two cassettes). Italian with English subtitles.

Most opera lovers are resigned to the probability that they will never see an ideal performance of *Macbeth*—the work is too complicated and the vocal roles are too demanding. This production, however, comes very close. Though there is not an Italian in the cast, we are in for a pleasant surprise.

Kostas Paskalis in the title role is first vicious, then greedy, and ultimately pathetic—a fine actor who looks the part and sings expressively. The British soprano Josephine Barstow is demonic and wild as Lady Macbeth but keeps the vocal line under control, even singing every note of the difficult brindisi in the second act. Her sinister sleepwalking scene lingers in the viewer's mind long after it's over. *Brava!*

James Morris brings wisdom and a handsome tone to Banquo's music, and Keith Erwen is a sincere, if not very Italianate, Macduff. The sparse sets are almost nonexistent, but the lighting—always important in this

Kostas Paskalis as Macbeth in the Glyndebourne Festival production of Verdi's opera. Courtesy Video Artists International.

opera—works wonders. The witches' scenes are remarkably eerie, and the whole mood and feel of this production are just right.

John Pritchard and his forces cannot be praised highly enough. This is a gem for lovers of Verdi and Shakespeare alike.

■ **Puccini:** *Madama Butterfly*

Raina Kabaivanska, Nazzareno Antinori, Eleanora Jankovic, Lorenzo Saccomani; Orchestra and chorus of the Arena di Verona, Maurizio Arena, cond.

HBO Video, color, 1983, 150 minutes. Italian with English subtitles.

■ **Puccini:** *Madama Butterfly*

Yasuko Hayashi, Peter Dvorsky, Hak Nam Kim, Giorgio Zancanaro; Orchestra and Chorus of La Scala, Milan, Lorin Maazel, cond.

Home Vision, color, 1986, 150 minutes. Italian with English subtitles.

These two performances of *Madama Butterfly* are perfect examples of how and how not to produce an opera, voices notwithstanding.

The HBO Video tape stars Raina Kabaivanska, a Bulgarian soprano known and admired the world over as a fine singing actress. Although a bit mature for Butterfly, and lacking the right timbre (the notorious Slavic vocal edge is out of place with Puccini's geisha), she offers a performance of exquisite tenderness and beauty. The rest of the cast is not up to her standards. Antinori uses his rather ordinary voice inexpressively as Pinkerton, Eleonora Jankovic is an acceptable but indifferent Suzuki, and Lorenzo Saccomani bullies his way through the part of Sharpless. But the singing is not the problem, for a great Butterfly should be able alone to carry the opera unless too many other things are working against her.

In this case, what works against Kabaivanska is the Arena di Verona. This is a sad opera about a small, exquisite character who goes from ecstasy to suicide in less than three hours, and we must get as close to her as possible to feel her anguish. We at home get closer than anyone in the arena, but unfortunately the company does not design its productions for the small screen. Watching this work, it is also easy to see why *Aïda, Turandot, Otello,* and *La Gioconda* are repertory staples in Verona: they are huge operas.

For this production, designer Ulisse Santicchi is to be commended for practically recreating Nagasaki, hills and all, and for designing a home for Butterfly that could probably house the current population of Kyoto. But it doesn't work for the opera's intimate theme; we always feel distanced. Even the remarkable Brian Large, who directed for TV, is at a loss. Unless he is working with extreme close-ups, which become tiresome, one gets the impression of gazing through the wrong end of a pair of binoculars. Furthermore, because the singers must impress people sitting several hundred feet away, they use very broad gestures, and the overall effect is like a silent movie. Conductor Maurizio Arena leads the Verona orchestra efficiently and with grand sweep, in keeping with the mood. Kabaivanska or not—and she *is* a great singer—this show is a failure, at least on the small screen.

By comparison, we have the La Scala performance. It helps the illusion that the two leading women are Orientals, though it's not necessary for an Otello or Aïda to be black or an Isolde to be Irish to make a convincing portrayal. What matters here is that the opera is offered in a space that allows it to unfold naturally, and that both designer Ichiro Takada and director Keita Asari have a sense of the work's intimacy and privacy.

Here the stage at La Scala is drastically raked and almost bare—very impressionistic and Japanese. Butterfly and her friends enter in silhouette, shielded shyly by their pastel umbrellas. Movement is held to a minimum except for Sharpless and Pinkerton, the two Yankees. The fragility of the fifteen- and then eighteen-year-old heroine can be gauged by her tiny movements: although Yasuko Hayashi is not small, she is made to appear very vulnerable. And when Butterfly commits *seppuku* attended by four obedient handmaidens, the tragedy—both cultural and personal—hits home.

The odd thing about this production is that neither Hayashi nor Hak Nam Kim as Suzuki is vocally very appealing. They certainly don't offend, but their voices do not make much of an impression. Peter Dvorsky is a shiny-toned rake of a Pinkerton who shows genuine remorse in the last act; Giorgio Zancanaro's Sharpless is sympathetic and more than attractively sung. Lorin Maazel squeezes every bit of poignancy out of the La Scala orchestra and chorus.

Though not an ideal performance of *Madama Butterfly,* the production has the right feel and look to it. It makes us live the experience. Verona's simply does not.

Raina Kabaivanska in the title role of the Arena di Verona production of Puccini's *Madama Butterfly*. Photo by Zoë Dominic. Courtesy HBO Video.

■ Puccini: *Manon Lescaut*

Kiri Te Kanawa, Placido Domingo, Thomas Allen, Forbes Robinson; the Royal Opera Chorus and the Orchestra of the Royal Opera House, Covent Garden, Giuseppe Sinopoli, cond. Directed by Götz Friedrich; designed by Günther Schneider-Siemssen. Directed for television by Humphrey Burton.

HBO Video, color, 1983, 130 minutes. Italian with English subtitles.

■ Puccini: *Manon Lescaut*

Renata Scotto, Placido Domingo, Pablo Elvira, Renato Capecchi; Chorus and Orchestra of the Metropolitan Opera House, James Levine, cond. Directed by Gian Carlo Menotti; designed by Desmond Heeley. Directed for television by Kirk Browning.

Paramount Home Video, color, 1980, 135 minutes. Italian with English subtitles.

These two performances, taped almost three years and an ocean apart, have more in common than their music and libretto. They both boast opulent and handsome productions, impressive directorial talents, well-known conductors, interesting divas in the title role, and Placido Domingo as Des Grieux. Oddly, one is effective theatre and the other is not.

The Met's performance, taped in 1980, has Renata Scotto as Manon. The soprano is in secure fine voice, despite a ragged high C or two. Scotto cajoles, pleads, wheedles, and dotes, and her interpretation, both vocally and histrionically, is absolutely believable; her death scene is truly distressing. One of Scotto's greatest talents is her ability to react to the other characters as if she hadn't been rehearsing with them for weeks, and that spontaneity is here as well.

The role of Des Grieux is long, high, loud, and dramatically draining, but Domingo copes with the vocal demands easily and acts naturally and convincingly. He's in excellent vocal shape, but one wishes he were capable of singing at a level below *forte* once in a while. Baritone Pablo Elvira is a better-than-usual Lescaut, and James Levine leads an exciting performance. TV director Kirk Browning milks all of the pathos out of Puccini's first great success by focusing on the sad-faced Scotto and the desperate Domingo, particularly in the opera's second half. Otherwise he's satisfied to allow us to see how handsome this production is.

The Covent Garden performance, too, has its good points, although director Götz Friedrich sees Manon as a petulant, grasping, and selfish liar. Geronte, here played by Forbes Robinson, is also repulsive, and Manon treats him with genuine scorn. Des Grieux is cast as a victim. Günther Schneider-Siemssen's sets are splendid, except for the final, Louisiana act, which looks more like one of the *Ring* cycle's more barren landscapes.

Domingo is again spectacular; indeed, his two performances are almost identical, down to the occasional strain on the same notes. Thomas Allen is vocally secure but a cunning and less likable Lescaut.

Kiri Te Kanawa is not quite Manon. In addition to not being in particularly gleaming voice (a rarity for this singer), with some real insecurity and shortness of breath during the first two acts, she is dramatically not up to the role's requirements. She was singing Manon for the first time (the prompter can often be heard, and she rarely takes her eyes off the conductor), and the close-ups reveal her doing what she's told, carefully awaiting each cue. As a result, there's no energy in her well-rehearsed but empty reading. Nor does conductor Giuseppe Sinopoli help with his odd choices of tempi. Manon's great final solo, "Sola, perduta, abbandonata," is taken much too slowly, and Te Kanawa looks as if she wishes it would end so she could go home.

This opera needs a great soprano, tenor, and conductor—and they all have to be equally great. Domingo remains the same, but the other two are winners in the Met production and problems at Covent Garden. The latter is far from a loser, but since we have a choice, it's clearly the Domingo, Scotto, Levine version.

Kiri Te Kanawa in a scene from the Royal Opera production of Puccini's *Manon Lescaut*. Photo by Catherine Ashmore. Courtesy HBO Video.

■ Donizetti: *Mary Stuart*

Janet Baker, Rosalind Plowright, David Rendall, Alan Opie, John Tomlinson; English National Opera Orchestra and Chorus, Charles Mackerras, cond.

HBO Video, color, 1982, 138 minutes. English. Libretto included.

Janet Baker chose *Maria Stuarda* (in an English translation by Tom Hammond) in which to take leave of the operatic stage; this performance was taped live at the London Coliseum in 1982. The libretto for this 1834 work is based on a tragedy by Schiller, in which Mary Stuart and Queen Elizabeth I confront each other in a park near Fotheringay Castle. Mary wins the battle but loses the war—along with her head—but not until she has gotten to curse the Queen, to pray to her maker for forgiveness, and to sing a lovely farewell to the earthly life in a lengthy final scene.

Originally composed for soprano, the title role is a great challenge. Sutherland, Sills, and Caballé, among very few others, have tried it in this century. By skillfully transposing parts of the opera down a whole tone or semitone, Janet Baker has suited the role perfectly to her mezzo-

Alan Opie (left) as Sir William Cecil, Rosalind Plowright as Queen Elizabeth I, and David Rendall as the Earl of Leicester in a scene from the English National Opera production of Donizetti's *Mary Stuart*. Photo by Catherine Ashmore. Courtesy HBO Video.

soprano voice, and none of it is beyond her. Mary is proud, angry, loving, and devout, and Baker misses not a twist of feeling, a turn of emotion, or a note along the way. It is a deeply realized portrayal.

Soprano Rosalind Plowright, looking properly dowdy and spiteful as Queen Elizabeth, sings with a voice-wrecking energy that is thrilling, though her English is rarely understandable. Tenor David Rendall makes the most of the forgettable role of Leicester, and bass John Tomlinson's Talbot is a comforting presence in Mary's confession scene. Alan Opie aids and abets Elizabeth with proper cunning as Cecil.

The production by Desmond Heeley is wonderful, and John Copley's direction, particularly in the second-act confrontation scene, is fast and furious. Charles Mackerras leads the ENO's forces well, with great understanding of its human drama. The entire show, however, is Janet Baker's. She should not be missed.

■ Cimarosa: *Il Matrimonio Segreto*

Carlos Feller, Barbara Daniels, David Kuebler, Marta Szirmay, Claudio Nicolai, Georgina Resick; Orchestra of the Drottning-holm Court Theatre, Stockholm, Hilary Griffiths, cond.

Home Vision, color, 1986, 150 minutes. Italian with English subtitles.

Long on charm but short on action, *Il Matrimonio Segreto* needs six committed singers and a director who takes the comic plot seriously and without exaggeration to make it effective. All these ingredients are here. Director Michael Hampe plays it as a story that could actually happen, and the acting is spirited and convincing. The simple, well-lighted set by Jan Schlubach works well, and the cast is up to its assignments.

The score itself is filled with felicities: the ingenious buffo duet at the start of the second act; the lively duet between Fidalma (Szirmay) and Paolino (Kuebler) that turns into a trio with Carolina (Resick); and the colorful orchestration throughout. The Drottningholm Court Theatre's orchestra plays beautifully on original instruments; in fact, watching the overture is one of this tape's highlights.

Both Barbara Daniels and Georgina Resick are excellent, although in different ways. The former's sound is more mellow, the latter's has a not uninteresting edge that is used to add piquancy to her characterization. Marta Szirmay, as Fidalma, has a dreadful voice, but it fits in nicely with the character she is portraying. David Kuebler has a clean-edged sound and can handle the role's coloratura, but he tends to attack phrases from a slightly flat vantage point.

The goings-on are dominated, as they should be, by Carlos Feller, who makes Geronimo less of a fool than usual; for once, Geronimo's attempts to marry Elisetta (Daniels) off to the wealthy Count Robinson are seriously portrayed. His restraint makes Geronimo come to life, and his voice always pleases. As Count Robinson, Claudio Nicolai lacks resonance but puts in a good performance nonetheless. In short, the ensemble work is what makes this production. Director Michael Hampe and conductor Hilary Griffiths are to be congratulated. Unfortunately, the voices are slightly out of sync with the tape most of the time.

■ Handel: *Messiah*

Sylvia McNair, Marietta Simpson, Jon Humphrey, William Stone; Atlanta Symphony Orchestra and Chamber Chorus, Robert Shaw, cond.

VAI, color, 1987, 141 minutes. English.

This is a handsome, dignified, all-purpose *Messiah* conducted by a master. It will remind listeners and viewers of how this work used to sound before the Hogwood, Parrott, Pinnock, and other "authentic" interpretations became popular. To be sure, there are faults in this performance, but it's a success nonetheless.

The work is given complete, with an orchestra and chorus of about fifty each. The chorus is so good that its bulk does not interfere with the performance—listen, for example, to "All we like sheep," the *Hallelujah* chorus, and the final "Amen." All of these are jaunty and lean, avoiding any Beechamesque bombast. (It can be argued that Shaw has picked up some of the best interpretive habits of the early music conductors.) The harpsichord, expertly played by Layton James, is always audible (kudos to engineer John McClure), despite Shaw's Mozart-size forces.

Where this production does fall short is in the solo singing. None of it is disgraceful and some of it is good—Sylvia McNair shines, for example—but others sound as if they might as well be singing a shopping list, so uninterested and remote are they. Jon Humphrey is a fine tenor, with impressive breath control, but except in "Thou shalt break them" he sounds almost as bored as mezzo Marietta Simpson does throughout.

Bass William Stone would be better suited to Verdi or Puccini—his is a good voice in the wrong part.

The orchestra plays beautifully, the camerawork is straightforward and direct, there's no attempt at artiness, and the sound is first-rate. This is clearly a *Messiah* for nonspecialists, but specialists can always turn to Christopher Hogwood's superb, if chilly, performance on HBO Video. What we have here is a solid reading with few surprises and some competent if not terribly inspired soloists. As such, it is recommended.

■ Britten: *A Midsummer Night's Dream*

James Bowman, Ileana Cotrubas, Cynthia Buchan, Felicity Lott, Ryland Davies, Dale Duesing, Curt Appelgren, Damien Nash, other soloists; the Glyndebourne Chorus and London Philharmonic Orchestra, Bernard Haitink, cond.

Home Vision, color, 1982, approx 150 minutes (two cassettes). English.

From the opening string glissandos of this, Britten's most otherworldly opera, one feels transported; rarely has orchestral tone painting set a mood so quickly and effectively. Without overstating the case, *A Midsummer Night's Dream* is (with the exception of Verdi's *Otello* and *Falstaff*) the finest operatic adaptation of Shakespeare in the repertory. It is to be savored, as is this beautiful Glyndebourne production.

The world of Oberon, Titania, and Puck is represented by the higher, sharper colors in the orchestra; the mortals are accompanied and identified by more down-to-earth instrumentation. Similarly, Oberon is sung by a countertenor, Titania by a coloratura soprano, and Puck is spoken by a preadolescent boy, while the earthlings range from baritone to bass.

John Bury's production mirrors the music, with sets and an atmosphere adapted to the inhabitants: misty and moonlighted for the fairy sequences, a wooded clearing in natural daylight for the mortals. (Robert Bryan and Bill Burgess are the lighting wizards.) Trees move mysteriously, Puck wears a red fright wig and flies in and out on branches, Titania and Oberon are dressed in deep blue with white hair and pointy ears. TV producer Dave Heather and stage director Peter Hall have created a truly dreamlike *Dream*.

The cast is first-rate. James Bowman uses his peculiar countertenor to create a malevolent Oberon to Ileana Cotrubas's eloquent Titania. All four of the young lovers are excellent, particularly Felicity Lott's exquisite Helena and Ryland Davies' suave yet desperate Lysander. Damien Nash speaks Puck's lines Cockney-style as if he were born to them. Curt Appelgren sings Bottom's music almost too elegantly; he could have been earthier. Conductor Haitink's slow tempi allows us to hear the sometimes startling orchestral textures, but the play scene could have used a more sprightly pacing. Sadly, the English diction of the upper voices is a chore to understand, but one can't have everything.

Petty carping aside, this is a superb performance. Even if twentieth-century opera isn't to your liking, you should know *A Midsummer Night's Dream*. Grab this one.

■ Gilbert and Sullivan: *The Mikado*

Marie Baron, Eric Donkin, Henry Ingram, Richard McMillan, Christina James, Gidon Saks; Orchestra and Chorus of the Stratford Festival, Berthold Carrière, cond. Directed and choreographed by Brian Macdonald.

Connaisseur (distributed by Home Vision), color, 1986, 150 minutes. English.

■ Gilbert and Sullivan: *The Gondoliers*

Douglas Chamberlain, Eric Donkin, John Keane, Paul Massell, Richard McMillan; Orchestra and Chorus of the Stratford Festival, Berthold Carrière, cond. Directed and choreographed by Brian Macdonald.

Connaisseur (distributed by Home Vision), color, 1986, 154 minutes. English.

■ Gilbert and Sullivan: *Iolanthe*

Maureen Forrester, Eric Donkin, Marie Baron, Paul Massell, Katharina Megli, Stephen Beamish; Orchestra and Chorus of the Stratford Festival, Berthold Carrière, cond. Directed and choreographed by Brian Macdonald.

Home Vision, color, 1988, 138 minutes. English.

A quick glance at the timings for these tapes reveals part of the problem: the conductor, Berthold Carrière, has added to and rearranged the music, and there are reams of additional dialogue, most of it designed to update and "make relevant" much of W. S. Gilbert's libretto. Some of the added dialogue is meant just to be funny (as if Gilbert were a tragedian), such as when the Duke of Plaza-Toro, in *The Gondoliers*, says, "It's enough to make a Venetian blind!" If your funny bone remains untickled by that, the rest of the "jokes" on these tapes will send you screaming.

As if that were not irritating enough, all the music is prerecorded, whereas the dialogue is spoken live. This leads to the conclusion that the laughter on these tapes is canned or, at least, sounds canned. And the cast mugs mercilessly. There is no reason for the Duchess of Plaza-Toro to be played by a man (this certainly was not in Gilbert and Sullivan's instructions), nor is Pooh-Bah in *The Mikado* supposed to be completely effeminate. In making these and other such decisions, director-choreographer Brian Macdonald reveals that he has little or no respect for these masterpieces of comic operetta. Real Savoyards, beware. Much of what you'll see here will enrage you.

Nonetheless, some of the singing is quite respectable, if never really idiomatic. In *Mikado*, Marie Baron is a lovely Yum-Yum, Christina James is a top-notch Katisha, and the men's chorus is excellent. The costumes are stunning, and the ingenious unit set consists of a series of movable wooden platforms on a wooden floor, with the background of a huge Oriental fan. Much of the added dialogue makes fun of Japanese accents, though, and the electronic audience applauds about every two minutes.

The Gondoliers suffers in many of the same ways, and the prancing and posturing are hard to watch without cringing. However, the sets and costumes are again very good, and the singing is above average. With the exception of Eric Donkin as the Duke and Richard McMillan as the Grand Inquisitor, whose clownish antics ruin both performances, the cast is excellent. The Palmieri Brothers are energetically sung by John Keane and Paul Massell, and all of the women shine. The chorus is superb. As usual, Brian Macdonald's ideas are good, but he beats them to death.

Iolanthe, the company's most recent production, is also badly overdone. It's presented as a touring company's one-night stand, complete with flirting stagehands and simpering chorus girls. Nevertheless, the production almost succeeds simply because this is Sullivan's most beautiful score, and the orchestra plays handsomely. The cast's diction is exemplary (true of all three productions), so that we can clearly hear the updated references to war in the Falklands, hockey player Wayne

Gretzky, and Margaret Thatcher. The tape is almost worth owning, too, for Maureen Forrester's Queen of the Fairies. Although she exaggerates the grande dame bit, she does contribute some desperately needed class to the show. The Lord Chancellor's nightmare song, sung by Eric Donkin, is also great fun.

What is infuriating about all three tapes is that so much care has been lavished on intolerable adaptations of these classic operettas. The general quality of production, the sound and color, and the energy level are very high. But during the quieter moments we can hear Gilbert and Sullivan turning over in their graves.

■ Verdi: *Nabucco*

Renato Bruson, Ghena Dimitrova, Dimiter Petkov, Bruna Baglioni, Ottavio Garaventa, soloists; Chorus and Orchestra of the Arena di Verona, Maurizio Arena, cond.

HBO Video, color, 1981, 132 minutes. Italian with English subtitles.

Nabucco, Verdi's third opera, catapulted him to fame. Part of the reason for its success was extramusical. At the time of its presentation in 1842, parts of Italy were tightly in the grip of Austria; and since the opera takes place during the Babylonian captivity of the Jews, there were many political parallels to be drawn. The great third-act chorus, "Va, pensiero," is ostensibly a prayer by the Hebrews for their lost homeland, and it struck a nationalistic chord in Italian hearts. But politics aside, much of *Nabucco* contains thrilling music, and here the performances of the two leading roles more than satisfy.

The eponymous hero is sung by baritone Renato Bruson, and his portrayal is complete, ranging from grandeur to tragedy, from victimizer to victim to hero. His tone is handsome throughout—menacing, touching, and heroic by turns. As Nabucco's evil daughter, Abigaille, Ghena Dimitrova sails through the difficult music with such authority that one might think it's easy. Indeed, with the possible exception of Lady Macbeth, this is Verdi's most brutal soprano role, requiring two-octave leaps, dazzling agility, endless power, and the ability to spin a soft, legato line. Dimitrova has it all, and she's astonishing.

Ottavio Garaventa and Bruna Baglioni, in relatively minor roles, are serviceable; bass Dimiter Petkov, however, in the key role of the priest

Zaccaria, is woolly when he should be authoritative. The sets and costumes are so silly (lampshade headgear, *Star Wars* outfits) that one has to chuckle, and Maurizio Arena leads an energetic if occasionally ragged performance. Nonetheless, this is an exciting performance of a somewhat neglected work and is highly recommended.

Renato Bruson in the title role of the La Scala production of Verdi's *Nabucco*. Photo by Lelli & Masotti. Courtesy HBO Video.

■ Gluck: *Orfeo ed Euridice*

Janet Baker, Elizabeth Gale, Elisabeth Speiser, soloists; the London Philharmonic Orchestra and the Glyndebourne Chorus, Raymond Leppard, cond.

Home Vision, color, 1982, 130 minutes. Italian with English subtitles.

Christoph Willibald von Gluck was a musical revolutionary. Tired of the popular operas that allowed singers to improvise and made no dramatic sense, he composed works in which the voice and orchestra were equals, works that were noble expressions of feelings as told through musical means. Difficult though it is to believe, the controversy between partisans of the "old" and "new" types of operas reached such a pitch in Paris in 1773 that duels were fought and lives lost.

At any rate, this is an utterly magnificent performance of the work that started it all. The classic story of the musician Orpheus, who descends into hell to retrieve his dead bride, Eurydice, and bring her back to life has often been treated by composers, but this 1762 telling is by far the most famous. This production was taped at the Glyndebourne Festival in 1982. Directed by Peter Hall in one of his truly brilliant moments and designed by John Bury, this is a stunning neoclassical production that looks as fine as it sounds. The red tones of hell, with a chorus of apelike damned clawing at the gates, contrast sharply with the blue silk of the Elysian Fields, and the stage movement (credited to Stuart Hopps—it seems more like choreography) is elegant and natural. The role of Amor is well rendered by the lovely Elizabeth Gale. Euridice is sung by Swiss soprano Elisabeth Speiser in a strong characterization that turns the mythic bride into a real person, sweet of tone and quite moving.

But overall, the show is Janet Baker's. In the trouser role of Orfeo she is expressive, musically dazzling (in the impossibly difficult aria that closes the first act), and touching throughout.

The chorus sings (and moves) superbly, and the orchestral playing makes us grateful for Gluck's revolutionary ideas. Raymond Leppard is a fine conductor, and this is one of his best achievements. Both picture and sound are good, and the subtitles are clean and clear. This production can't be recommended highly enough. It is rare indeed to find an operatic milestone so perfectly served.

■ Verdi: *Otello*

Vladimir Atlantov, Kiri Te Kanawa, Piero Cappuccilli, other soloists; Orchestra and Chorus of the Arena di Verona, Zoltan Pesko, cond.

HBO Video, color, 1982, 145 minutes. Italian with English subtitles.

The finest performance on this tape is Kiri Te Kanawa's as Desdemona. She looks beautiful, is in excellent voice, and her portrayal of Otello's falsely accused wife is expressive and touching. Tenor Vladimir Atlantov, after singing consistently flat during the first act, comes into his own in his somewhat hysterical third act, but by then any effect he might have conveyed has been lost. Atlantov's voice is an admirable instrument, but here he doesn't always have it under control. Cappuccilli as Iago has plenty of voice but little sublety. Pesko has a hard time keeping the Arena's forces in line; the chorus is ragged and the orchestra sounds at times like a high school band.

The sets and costumes, all in whites and golds, are dazzling, and the director (and the TV director Preben Montell) make sense of both the crowd scenes and the more intimate moments.

In short, this *Otello* is far from perfect but is worth viewing, particularly for Te Kanawa's Desdemona.

■ Verdi: *Otello*

Hans Nöcker, Christa Noack-Von Kamptz, Vladimir Bauer, soloists; the Berlin Komische Oper, Kurt Masur, cond. Directed by Walter Felsenstein.

View Video, color, 1969, 121 minutes. German with English subtitles.

This film is in glorious, vivid color, and there the praise must end; the famous German stage director Walter Felsenstein is clearly done in by his cast and conductor. There isn't an idiomatic performance on the tape, and conductor Masur has chosen such fast tempi that the acts whiz by and all memory of them fades instantly. Moreover, the lurching, bellowing, and posing of the cast would not be out of place in a silent film. This tape may eventually become a "camp" collector's item, but it is a crime against Verdi.

■ Britten: *Peter Grimes*

Jon Vickers, Heather Harper, Norman Bailey, Patricia Payne, Marilyn Hill Smith, Anne Pashley, Elizabeth Bainbridge, John Dobson, Philip Gelling, other soloists; the Orchestra and Chorus of the Royal Opera House, Covent Garden, Colin Davis, cond.

HBO Video, color, 1981, 155 minutes. English.

A great performance of this work in the opera house can leave the audience emotionally shattered, and this cassette comes as close as possible to providing that experience. Premiered in 1945, *Peter Grimes* was an immediate success. Indeed, the British were convinced that English opera, which had been considered moribund since Thomas Arne, was alive and well after all. They were, it turns out, quite right.

Britten got his idea from a work by a minor poet, "The Borough" by George Crabbe. He found the character of the sadistic fisherman, Peter Grimes, whom the villagers despise for his "differences," fascinating and operatically interesting. Britten and his librettist Montagu Slater turned the fisherman into a lonely, disturbing, sympathetic outsider whose words and music tell us more about his state of mind than we ever learn from the poem. That the opera shocks was undeniable from the beginning; that it is a masterpiece of dramatic construction has taken time to acknowledge.

This production documents one of the legendary performances of our time. So sad, so moving, so impulsive is Vickers' Peter Grimes that we are more than touched: we are overwhelmed. Vocally, the tenor has always been problematic. The sheer size of his voice is staggering. Where other tenors have problems, Vickers sails through and vice versa—but it

Heather Harper and Andrew Wilson in a scene from the Royal Opera production of Britten's *Peter Grimes*. Photo by Clive Barda. Courtesy HBO Video.

doesn't matter. As an actor, Vickers is just as great. Will any Grimes ever be better? Most critics doubt it.

The remainder of the cast is Covent Garden, vintage 1981, at its best. Heather Harper is a wonderfully sympathetic Ellen, the widow with whom Grimes wants to build a life, and Norman Bailey is a kindly, fine-grained Balstrode. Elizabeth Bainbridge, Marilyn Hill Smith, and Anne Pashley are outstanding, and Patricia Payne's Mrs. Sedley is easy to ridicule but a viciously dangerous character. The others in the cast define the word "ensemble," aided by Elijah Moshinsky's understanding directorial hand. (John Vernon directs for TV and knows just where to point his camera to emphasize a situation.) Colin Davis and the Covent Garden musicians cannot be praised highly enough, nor can the chorus, the true star of this opera.

Any opera collection without this tape is woefully incomplete.

■ Stravinsky: *The Rake's Progress*

Leo Goeke, Samuel Ramey, Felicity Lott, Rosalind Elias, Richard van Allan, other soloists; London Philharmonic Orchestra and Glyndebourne Festival Chorus, Bernard Haitink, cond.

VAI, color, 1977, 146 minutes (two cassettes). English.

This opera tells an unpleasant and sinister story and there's no beauty in the score, but a good performance of it can be very effective, and this one is superb.

After its premiere in Venice in 1951, *The Rake's Progress* was quickly staged by many other major opera houses, almost invariably to negative reviews. It has, however, become a repertory staple in many companies, and in this production, taped at Glyndebourne, designer David Hockney has created a childlike world with bright sunny colors and troubled overtones, just right for this wryly cynical work. Director John Cox is of like mind, and it works.

Tenor Leo Goeke is splendid in the role of Tom Rakewell, a combination of stupidity and blind ambition. Samuel Ramey plays Nick Shadow (a/k/a the devil), and even in 1977 a great future was in evidence. Total commitment, deep, resonant sound, and an eye for evil make this a valuable portrayal. Felicity Lott is bit too mature for Anne Trulove (the woman Tom is supposed to marry before he is corrupted and takes up with a bearded lady), but she sings well and with fine diction. Rosalind Elias sings Baba the Turk (the aforementioned bearded lady) with all her heart and just a touch of repulsiveness. Richard van Allan is excellent as Anne's father, as is the rest of the cast.

Haitink and the Glyndebourne forces give their all and come close to making a case for this difficult, unsonorous work. And if it's one of your favorites, you won't find a better production.

■ Verdi: *Requiem*

Margaret Price, Jessye Norman, José Carreras, Ruggero Raimondi; London Symphony Orchestra, Edinburgh Festival Chorus, Claudio Abbado, cond.

HBO Video, color, 1982, 112 minutes. Latin, no subtitles.

At first glance, the Verdi *Requiem* doesn't seem like a natural for videocassette, although Verdi's mass was often criticized as far too operatic for liturgical services. And, indeed, although Edinburgh's Usher Hall is a handsome building, and the audience and participants are interesting to observe, the visual aspects do pall after about a half hour. Fortunately, this is a beautiful, well-integrated performance, and the listener-viewer can concentrate on the music alone.

By 1982, Abbado had already proven himself a superb conductor of Verdi. Here he leads the performance with strength, control, and the full range of expression Verdi required, with markings from *ppppp* to *ff* scrupulously observed. The Edinburgh Festival Chorus and London Symphony Orchestra follow Abbado's lead diligently, singing and playing with great energy and tonal luster. The "Dies irae" is properly thundering, the "Hostias" appropriately reverent.

For the most part, the soloists are above average. The soprano Margaret Price has a meltingly lovely tone, warm and bright by turns, and a real trill. She lacks the chest voice for a few moments in "Libera me" but is otherwise ideal. The same goes for Jessye Norman, here singing the mezzo part (though she would be just as comfortable with the soprano). Her control and unbroken register are a joy. José Carreras, in superb voice (shortness of breath at the close of the "Ingemisco" notwithstanding), varies his dynamics to the letter of the composer's instructions—his *pianissimo* at the start of the "Hostias" is truly memorable. Only bass Ruggero Raimondi seems to be overstretched. His burnished tone is taxed by the dramatic demands of the music, and he tends to sing sharp and force too often. Still, he holds up well in the ensembles.

This is a fine choice, then. John Drummond, the festival's director, unnecessarily gives a lengthy introduction, but the music's the thing, and it's very well played and sung here.

■ Monteverdi: *The Return of Ulysses to His Homeland*

Janet Baker, Benjamin Luxon, Anne Howells, Ian Caley, Richard Lewis, Alexander Oliver, Robert Lloyd, Ugo Trama, soloists; the London Philharmonic Orchestra and Glyndebourne Chorus, Raymond Leppard, cond.

VAI, color, 1973, 152 minutes (two cassettes). Italian with English subtitles.

The Return of Ulysses, first performed in 1641, is the second of Claudio Monteverdi's three surviving operas. It lacks the innocence and purity of his *Orfeo* and the sensuousness of his *L'Incoronazione di Poppea*, but it is captivating in its truthfulness, sadness, and ultimately, its joy. The performance on these cassettes is warm and honest; it's hard to imagine a better one.

Since Monteverdi left much of the scoring incomplete, conductor Raymond Leppard has updated it by a respectable fifty or so years. Peter Hall's directorial eye has rarely been sharper, and John Bury's classical sets are simple but colorful. Together with the large cast, they tell the touching story of the faithful Penelope, who awaits and is finally reunited with her Ulysses. There are occasional cuts in the score, and some purists may not approve of them or of Leppard's orchestration, but others will find little or nothing to offend.

Baritone Benjamin Luxon is a virile, natural Ulysses, singing easily and acting with conviction. As his faithful shepherd, Eumetes, Richard Lewis uses his expressive tenor to great advantage, as does Ian Caley as Telemachus. Anne Howells as Minerva and Robert Lloyd as Neptune are properly godlike and resonant and draw fine characterizations.

Janet Baker's exemplary interpretation of Penelope portrays her as dignified, resolute, and loving. When she finally realizes that Ulysses has returned, we cannot help but be moved. Her voice is sensual, full, sweet, and perfectly even throughout the scale.

This opera is not easy to digest—early music rarely is—but this tape makes it easy. We are lucky indeed to have this excellent performance available for home viewing.

■ Strauss: *Der Rosenkavalier*

Kiri Te Kanawa, Anne Howells, Barbara Bonney, Aage Haugland, Jonathan Summers, Robert Tear, Cynthia Buchan, Dennis O'Neill, other soloists; the Royal Opera Chorus and the Orchestra of the Royal Opera House, Covent Garden, Georg Solti, cond.

Home Vision, color, 1985, 204 minutes (two cassettes). German with English subtitles.

This *Rosenkavalier* is directed by filmmaker John Schlesinger, who made films such as *Marathon Man, The Day of the Locust, Midnight Cowboy,*

Janet Baker as Penelope in the Glyndebourne Festival production of Monteverdi's *The Return of Ulysses to His Homeland.* Courtesy Video Artists International.

and *Sunday, Bloody Sunday*. It's refreshing to see that he has a sense of fun that's neither forced nor vulgar, and allows the characters to develop naturally without resorting to unnecessary slapstick or exaggeration. Schlesinger also makes sure that Octavian is the centerpiece of the action, as he should be. Schlesinger racily allows lots of kissing, right on the lips, and it all seems natural, except occasionally in close-ups.

Kiri Te Kanawa as the Marschallin doesn't come close to Elisabeth Schwarzkopf in terms of insight or revealing moments. At the time of this filming, Kanawa was forty-one and six years closer to the Marschallin's age (thirty-two, according to Strauss) than was Schwarzkopf when she played the Marschallin in the von Karajan version. Nuances are not Te Kanawa's strong suit, so she doesn't capture the character's mature despair and sadness, either. Where the Marschallin should be scolding with Octavian, she is merely petulant; when she shows impatience with the Baron, she does so in a childish rather than aristocratic manner. But the camera loves her from all angles and distances, and her singing is so beautiful as to be dizzying—the great third-act trio is taken very slowly and is sustained exquisitely. And her reading of the role is valid, if a bit shallow and undefined.

The Octavian of Anne Howells is sensitive, intelligent, boyish, and finely tuned. Unfortunately, close-ups reveal her age and a certain awkwardness that a theatre audience would not necessarily notice. TV director Brian Large is sensitive to the many small details of characterization that make this work so special. Aage Haugland is a singing Baron Ochs, rather than a speaking one; he actually sings all the notes and still makes his effect. His Ochs is offensive and lecherous but never repulsive. Barbara Bonney, as Sophie, is perfect: pretty and blond; alternately naive, outraged, and radiantly surprised; and she and Howells react to each other with genuine emotion in the scene with the presentation of the silver rose. All of the smaller roles are well cast; Robert Tear is a slimy Valzacchi, and Dennis O'Neill nicely hams up the Italian tenor's aria (note Te Kanawa's attitude here as compared to Schwarzkopf's in the VAI tape).

Solti conducts masterfully, knowing when the score is meant to be earthy and rambunctious, and when to lushly highlight the wind instruments. He favors slow tempi throughout, which helps to make the action clearer. The balance between voices and orchestra is ideal.

William Dudley's sets are handsome, as are Maria Bjoernson's costumes. The prompter can often be heard—particularly cueing Te Kanawa—but no recording is without its flaws. Special praise is due for the intelligent, clear, and very helpful subtitles.

Despite the somewhat superficial characterization of Te Kanawa's Marschallin, the sheer beauty of her singing excuses almost every shortcoming.

■ Wagner: *Tannhäuser*

Richard Cassily, Eva Marton, Tatiana Troyanos, Bernd Weikl, John Macurdy; Metropolitan Opera Orchestra and Chorus, James Levine, cond.

Paramount Home Video, color, 1982, 176 minutes. German with English subtitles.

This performance, taped live at the Met, does not benefit from Richard Cassily's poor performance as Tannhäuser. Granted, the role is difficult, but Cassily actually loses his voice during the Rome narrative in the final act. His tone is nasal and unappealing, and his commitment to the part, though admirable, is small compensation. James Levine's pedestrian conducting is also a detriment. He keeps things moving, and the orchestra and chorus perform well, but there's no cumulative effect. Even the big second-act finale counts for nothing dramatically. Levine seems to misunderstand the opera, or else he just isn't interested. It's a rare lapse in this fine conductor's career.

Other than that, the cast performs well. Eva Marton is a big-voiced, clear, and sincere Eva, and Tatiana Troyanos is a ravishing, sensuous-sounding Venus. Bernd Weikl's Wolfram is excellent; John Macurdy's Landgraf is less so.

The star of the production is the production itself. The Venusberg has never been more alluring than in Günther Schneider-Siemssen's decor—natural yet fantastic—while the rest of the production remains firmly rooted in reality. Brian Large has directed for TV with sensitivity and attention to detail.

There probably won't be another *Tannhäuser* on videocassette for a long time, so this is the one to purchase.

■ Puccini: *Tosca*

Eva Marton, Giacomo Aragall, Ingvar Wixell; Orchestra and Chorus of the Arena di Verona, Daniel Oren, cond.

HBO Video, color, 1984, 126 minutes. Italian with English subtitles.

The Arena di Verona's huge stage is well used in this successful production of *Tosca*. Praise goes to Fiorenzo Giorgi for the handsome sets and costumes and to Silvano Bussotti for his intelligent direction. TV director Brian Large has compensated nicely for the vastness of the setting, and the opera transfers nicely to the small screen.

Eva Marton, in the title role, uses her formidable voice wisely and generously. Everything she does is right, but her reading is rather superficial. Tosca, after all, is a woman in conflict—devout, yet sensual and capable (much to her own horror) of murder. Marton only hints at these complexities of character, all the while singing with golden tone.

Giacomo Aragall possesses a beautiful tenor and sings the role of

Eva Marton as Tosca and Ingvar Wixell as Scarpia in the Arena di Verona production of Puccini's *Tosca*. Photo by Catherine Ashmore. Courtesy HBO Video.

Cavaradossi well. But he is hardly a great actor, and though his portrayal is adequate, it lacks presence and makes little impression. Ingvar Wixell is without the truly Italian sound needed for the role of Scarpia but offers a remarkable characterization. His is a truly sadistic Scarpia, menacing and cruel.

The conductor, Daniel Oren, does a good job if without much originality.

Recommended, with reservations.

■ Puccini: *Tosca*

Hildegard Behrens, Placido Domingo, Cornell MacNeil; Orchestra and Chorus of the Metropolitan Opera, Giuseppe Sinopoli, cond. Designed and directed by Franco Zeffirelli.

Paramount Home Video, color, 1985, 127 minutes. Italian with English subtitles.

Zeffirelli's gargantuan production of *Tosca* barely fits on the small screen—the remarkable (but unnecessary) scene change in the final act is not even seen—but the director for TV has done a good job. We don't get lost in the action, and the camera angles generally favor the singers. The action moves intelligently; the sets and costumes are appropriately opulent.

Hildegard Behrens' voice, Germanic sound, and delivery are not naturally suited to the role of Tosca, but she works to make it her own, and the result is a believable, understandable portrayal. Domingo is nearly perfect as Cavaradossi. His is a passionate portrayal, and he is in rock-solid voice throughout. He does tend, however, to sing much of the music at the same volume, which becomes tiring at times. Cornell MacNeil's Scarpia is ostensibly malevolent but hardly convincing. Moreover, by this point in his career his voice is threadbare and harsh. The rest of the cast is good, and Zeffirelli has given nice character touches to each minor player.

Giuseppe Sinopoli's conducting is taut and devoid of most of his usual eccentricities of tempi and volume. But though he allows the music to work its natural magic, he offers no new insights into the score. Although Behrens is not the ideal Tosca, this tape is recommended. By the end, one cannot help but be impressed by its vitality and sense of drama.

■ **Puccini:** *Il Trittico: Il Tabarro, Suor Angelica, and Gianni Schicchi*

Sylvia Sass, Nicola Martinucci, Piero Cappuccilli; Rosalind Plowright, Dunja Vejzovic; Juan Pons, Cecilia Gasdia, Yuri Marusin, Eleanora Jankovic; Orchestra and chorus of La Scala, Milan, Gianandrea Gavazzeni, cond.

Home Vision, color, 1983, 150 minutes. Italian with English subtitles.

Most critics agree that *Gianni Schicchi* is the masterpiece of Puccini's triple bill, faulting *Suor Angelica* for its sentimental story and consigning *Il Tabarro* to an undistinguished third place. But a strong case can be made for *Tabarro* as the composer's tightest, most brutal melodrama, capable of making a powerful impression on the listener.

Unfortunately, this production of the opera doesn't quite make it. In this 1983 taping from La Scala, conductor Gianandrea Gavazzeni seems out of his element in Puccini's veristic idiom and, throughout all three operas, leans toward too fast tempi. *Tabarro* suffers most, despite some committed singing and acting from the principals. Sylvia Sass engages in some unreliable vocalizing as Giorgetta but conveys a passionate tangle of emotions in this wonderfully tawdry tale. Nicola Martinucci is suitably heroic as her lover, Luigi; and Piero Cappuccilli broods and throbs as her husband. The remainder of the cast is suitably intense, as is Silvano Bussotti's direction. The sets, mostly painted flats, are dull and uninteresting.

Suor Angelica is not easy to stage successfully. It is about a young girl who has borne a child out of wedlock and entered a convent to atone for her sin, only to learn that the child has died. It needs vital singers in the title role and in the role of the aunt who asks Suor Angelica to sign over part of her estate and who reveals the truth about her child. Rosalind Plowright gives an excellent performance in the title role. Despite some avoidance of high notes, she makes this all-too-human drama come vividly to life. Dunja Vejzovich, however, lacks both the vocal weight and presence to make a suitably detached and hateful aunt.

Gianni Schicchi is the most successfully presented of the three operas. This tale, taken from a couplet in Dante's *Inferno,* is about a man who impersonates a dead man in order to trick his greedy relatives out of their inheritance. It requires great ensemble work as well as defined individual characterizations. Juan Pons as Schicchi sings all the notes without faking or mugging, and his portrayal is a total success. Young Cecilia Gasdia is lovely as his daughter Lauretta, and her "O mio babbino caro" is memorable and touching. Russian tenor Yuri Marusin, who looks and sounds as if he's only in his early twenties, exhibits a fine voice as Rinuccio but suffers from pitch problems. The relatives are appropriately grim and greedy, and conductor Gavazzeni is in good form, although at times, again, he seems to be in a hurry. Sets, costumes, and direction are excellent.

TV director Brian Large has relied somewhat heavily on close-ups throughout this trio of operas, and the lighting always seems a bit too bright. But, even with their problems, these performances are recommended. (Perhaps the Met's trio, starring Renata Scotto, may come out on videocassette one of these days. Comparing the two sets would be interesting.)

■ Verdi: *Il Trovatore*

Rosalind Plowright, Fiorenza Cossotto, Franco Bonisolli, Giorgio Zancanaro, Paolo Washington, soloists; Chorus and Orchestra of the Arena di Verona, Reynald Giovaninetti, cond.

Home Vision, color, 1985, 150 minutes. Italian with English subtitles.

This production of *Trovatore* doesn't look very good; there's scaffolding in almost every scene, half the chorus is in armor and the rest in red tunics, and there is much confused comings and goings on stage. Nonetheless, there are some real vocal thrills here.

British soprano Rosalind Plowright hurls herself both vocally and histrionically into the part of Leonora and, while her voice often sounds pushed to its limit, she keeps the energy level high. Fiorenza Cossotto, rightly acknowledged as one of the great Azucenas, does not disappoint. She delivers a fine, strong, melodramatic performance.

Tenor Franco Bonisolli's performance reflects an earlier, stodgy, stand-up-and-deliver kind of acting, and his singing hasn't a shred of subtlety or nuance. He encores "Di quella pira" before the audience asks him to, and he makes quite a noise.

By far the most polished, Verdian singing on this set comes from baritone Giorgio Zancanaro as di Luna. His suave, beautiful voice has a snarl in the vicious moments and a caress in the more tender ones. He tries to act, but in vain. Conductor Giovaninetti often takes his cues from his unruly soloists but keeps things moving and (almost) together. This performance is good fun, and if this is what you look for in a Verdi opera, this tape is for you.

■ Verdi: *Il Trovatore*

Joan Sutherland, Lauris Elms, Kenneth Collins, Jonathan Summers, Donald Shanks, soloists; the Elizabethan Sydney Orchestra and Australian Opera Chorus, Richard Bonynge, cond.

Sony, color, 1983, 138 minutes. Italian with English subtitles.

This release from Australia has clearly been built around its national treasure, Joan Sutherland. She embellishes Leonora's music throughout, and while some Verdi purists may be furious, her additions are both interesting and musical—particularly given this particular soprano's strong points. As the opera progresses, her singing takes on a real dramatic flair, and she comes into her own in the final act, infusing the music and situation with unexpected emotion. Sutherland's is a more dignified than passionate Leonora, but this should come as no surprise. She is unfortunately costumed in the first act like a mountain of sherbet, but as the evening moves along she wears more appropriate clothes.

Lauris Elms is a mezzo without a very interesting sound, but she manages to breathe life into Azucena despite Elijah Moshinsky's direction, which keeps her seated throughout the second act. (His weak staging does not help any of the singers.) The men in the cast fare the worst. Donald Shanks is an accurate if bored Ferrando, and despite his musicality, Jonathan Summers is a provincial di Luna. Kenneth Collins sounds desperate as Manrico, and he is clearly overtaxed. The sets are a series of paint smears, and the costumes have no relation to any particular period or locale.

Richard Bonynge leads a pretty performance devoid of dramatic content, and the orchestra plays well. The chorus sings in unidiomatic Italian. This is probably a must for Sutherland fans and a must-not for almost everyone else.

■ Puccini: *Turandot*

Ghena Dimitrova, Cecilia Gasdia, Nicola Martinucci, Graziano Olidori, Pier Francesco Poli, Antonio Bevacqua, Ivo Vinco, soloists; Orchestra and Chorus of the Arena di Verona, Maurizio Arena, cond.

HBO Video, color, 1983, 116 minutes. Italian with English subtitles.

This blazing and colorful, if interpretively bland, *Turandot* showcases Bulgarian soprano Ghena Dimitrova. Her voice, though not conventionally pretty, is awe-inspiring and has a cutting edge at the top that can startle and amaze. She is costumed here all in white, with long black hair—a dramatically effective image. For sheer power and some nice effects, Dimitrova is definitely worth seeing and hearing.

Her Calaf is Nicola Martinucci, as usual a fine, all-purpose tenor with a wonderfully free top voice (like Franco Corelli, he takes the optional high C in the second act). His acting is of the hand-to-heart school, but since nuances are not the order of the day in Verona, one doesn't mind. Cecilia Gasdia is a lovely young Liù. Ivo Vinco sings an impressive Timur, and the Ping, Pang, and Pong characters are sprightly and tuneful.

The handsome production is long on grandeur, and the intelligent camerawork helps us to pick out the principals among the throngs onstage. Maurizio Arena's conducting keeps things moving—no more, no less. This *Turandot* is a success and is recommended.

■ Puccini: *Turandot*

Eva Marton, Katia Ricciarelli, José Carreras, John Paul Bogart, other soloists; Orchestra and Chorus of the Vienna State Opera, Vienna Boys' Choir, Lorin Maazel, cond.

MGM/UA Home Video, color, 1983, 138 minutes. Italian with English subtitles.

Even if the singing and orchestral playing were not of a very high quality, this cassette would still have to be recommended. *Turandot*, Puccini's last opera, is here given a phantasmagoric production, abstractly designed by Timothy O'Brien and Tazeena Firth and directed by the estimable Hal Prince. Along with Lorin Maazel, they seem to realize that this is an impressionistic and surreal work, and they have created a physical and aural atmosphere that perfectly suits the music. Maazel's tempi are unusually slow, but this only serves to point up the many colors in the score. The whole effect is dreamlike—if not a bit nightmarish.

Unfortunately, Maazel's tempi put extra strain on the singers. Even the indefatigable Eva Marton in the title role seems as if she would be more comfortable with brisker tempi, but she nonetheless is convincing as the icy princess who melts for love. José Carreras turns Calaf into a real human being, and sings with a golden tone when the tempi aren't causing him to work too hard. Katia Ricciarelli, wearing a silly outfit, doesn't hit her stride until the final act, at which point she is very touching. John Paul Bogart is an acceptable Timur, and the remainder of the cast has been well rehearsed. The orchestra, chorus, and boys' choir are excellent. Picture and sound are also extraordinary, as is this whole concept—very high-tech and very daring. Don't miss this one.

■ Knussen: *Where the Wild Things Are*

Karen Beardsley, Andrew Gallacher, Hugh Hetherington, others; libretto by Maurice Sendak; designed by Maurice Sendak; directed and choreographed by Frank Corsaro; The London Sinfonietta, Oliver Knussen, cond.

Home Vision, color, 1985, 40 minutes. English, libretto included.

■ Knussen: *Higglety Pigglety Pop!*

Cynthia Buchan, Andrew Gallacher, Rosemary Hardy, Neil Jenkins, others; libretto by Maurice Sendak; designed by Maurice Sendak; directed and choreographed by Frank Corsaro; the London Sinfonietta, Oliver Knussen, cond.

Home Vision, color, 1985, 60 minutes. English, libretto included.

Oliver Knussen knows how to write operas for children that keep adults fascinated as well, and Maurice Sendak's wonderful sets and costumes practically steal the show. The great mystery, of course, is why Home Vision did not package these two delightful operas together. They're a perfect pair since they have the same composer-conductor, designer-librettist and director-choreographer—not to mention the same mood and tone. As consumers, most of us would be far more interested in buying one package instead of two, since it would be cheaper and more compact.

In *Wild Things*, a rambunctious little boy named Max is sent to bed without his dinner. His room is immediately transformed into a magic place, and he sails off to a land full of "wild things." While the wild things love Max so much that they want to eat him up, they eventually settle for crowning him their king. But Max suddenly feels hungry and goes home, where he finds that his mother has left him a nice dinner. The music is inventive, with a big percussion and wind section and vivid dramatic thrust. The big "wild things" (which look like singing and dancing pillows) are a joy. Karen Beardsley as Max has a lot of singing to do, and every note and word is clear. As always, Sendak is psychologically right on target, and so is Knussen.

Higglety Pigglety Pop! is a delight, too. A big, furry dog named Jennie (Cynthia Buchan) wants to travel the world to "find something more than everything." She's told that she can get a job with the World Mother Goose Theatre, and along the way she meets a cat who's a milkman, a cantankerous, tail-pulling baby, a lion, and an ash tree that bemoans the loss of its leaves (ingeniously scored for a tenor and a baritone singing simultaneously). She soon gets to the theatre and is named its leading lady. The opera has some beautiful, wistful passages as well as funny ones, and Knussen's idiom here borrows from Mozart, Debussy, and others—all to fine effect.

These two Glyndebourne productions are definitive. Both are worth the viewer's time (and money) and will keep both grown-ups and any child over six entertained. Highly recommended.

Opera: Film Versions

■ **Menotti: *Amahl and the Night Visitors***

Teresa Stratas, Robert Sapolsky, Giorgio Tozzi, Willard White, Nico Castel, Michael Lewis; Ambrosian Opera Chorus and Philharmonia Orchestra, Jesús López-Cobos, cond.

VAI, color, 1979, 52 minutes. English.

This opera, the first created for the small screen, was commissioned by NBC for their 1951 Christmas Eve telecast. The result was *Amahl and the Night Visitors*, a tale of a crippled boy who is miraculously healed after a visit from the Three Wise Men on their way to see the Christ child. The work instantly became a family favorite and is a seasonal staple in many of the world's great opera houses. A moving and somehow true-to-itself opera, its story has plenty of sentiment and slapstick combined with lush melodies and dramatic musical moments.

This performance was filmed in the Judean Hills of Israel and is not only visually attractive but also ably—even brilliantly—acted and sung. The mother and son roles are performed by the estimable Teresa Stratas and the young Robert Sapolsky. She is at her dramatic best, he is tonally pure and clear of diction. The Three Kings are well cast too, with special praise going to Willard White's Balthazar. Tozzi and Castel are fine as well, as Melchior and Kaspar. None of the cast indulges in stock operatic posing—this opera is played as a real drama.

Jesús López-Cobos conducts with warmth and understanding. However, the sound on the tape is far more distorted than one would expect. Don't let it deter you from enjoying this production, but it may be a problem for some.

■ Bizet: *Carmen*

Julia Migenes-Johnson, Placido Domingo, Faith Esham, Ruggero Raimondi; Orchestre National de France, Chorus and Children's Choir of Radio France; Lorin Maazel, cond. Directed by Francesco Rosi.

RCA/Columbia Pictures Home Video, color, 1984, 151 minutes. French with English subtitles.

The praises of this film have been widely sung by opera and movie fans alike, and it loses none of its luster when it is viewed on a small screen. It was filmed on location in Andalusia, and the stark beauty of the countryside and the opera's violent plot combine perfectly. The enthusiasm and involvement of principals and extras alike are a credit to director Rosi.

The film opens with the killing of a bull in a bullring, and from then on, we know what to expect. This *Carmen* is a sexy, violent affair, and the usually tame performances in the opera house will never measure up to this one.

Placido Domingo does not disappoint. His voice is free and ringing and once he is given something to do physically (Rosi apparently sees Don José as subdued but inherently violent, and the libretto backs him up here) his unbridled passion becomes terrifying. Ruggero Raimondi's Escamillo is a charismatic braggart, with plenty of swagger in both voice and strut. Faith Esham makes the most of Micaela. This is not a role that creates stars, but the soprano impresses in both her first-act duet with Domingo and her third-act aria.

All of this is gravy, of course. *Carmen* is only as good as its Carmen, and this film wins in that department as well. The soprano Julia Migenes-Johnson is a gutsy, insinuating, disturbingly sensual gypsy, and she sings the music easily. Self-assured and a pleasure to watch, hers is an exciting interpretation.

Lorin Maazel's pacing, aside from a too-slow Gypsy Song, is just right, and the muscular sound that he gets from the orchestra is very apt. The subtitles are better than most, and the entire production is authentically French, Spanish, cinematic, and operatic. It belongs in every collection.

■ The Charm of La Bohème

Jan Kiepura, Marta Eggerth. Music by Puccini and Robert Stolz.

Lyric Distribution, black & white, 1936, 95 minutes. German.

Best described as a piece of tragic fluff, this oddity is about a bunch of Bohemians, who have a lot of fun, and a sickly heroine diagnosed as having "atrophy of the lungs." Kiepura and Eggerth play two singers who are in love and want to sing in *La Bohème* together. No one mentions that the plot of the opera is the same as their lives in the film, to the point where the soprano actually dies onstage. Opera verité or kitsch—you'll have to decide.

Kiepura was a tenor with a fine technique, but he lacked the sweetness of tone to make it truly ingratiating. Here he sings "Che gelida manina," Rossini's "La Danza," and some dreadful ditties by Stolz, serving them all well. Eggerth sings "Mi chiamano Mimi" in German, with an invisible orchestra accompanying her in the middle of a zany, Bohemian party, and she later launches into Musetta's Waltz. Oddly, both arias sound much the same.

The film also contains plot elements of *La Traviata*, but it's doubtful that anyone will want to hear about them. In short, this one is so odd it's better left unseen. Recordings of Kiepura cost less and have far more satisfying music.

■ Mozart: *Don Giovanni*

Ruggero Raimondi, José Van Dam, John Macurdy, Edda Moser, Kenneth Riegel, Kiri Te Kanawa, Malcolm King; Orchestra and Chorus of the Paris Opera, Lorin Maazel, cond. Conceived by Rolf Leibermann; directed by Joseph Losey.

Kultur, color, 1978, 176 minutes. Italian with English subtitles.

In 1978, when this film was released in theatres, many people commented about two aspects of the movie that now seem unimportant: the decision on the part of the director to move the action to Venice, and the role of an omnipresent, young, good-looking valet in black who seems to have a great deal to do with the Don's actions. Since then, of course, we've had performances of *Don Giovanni* that take place in locales far less likely than Venice, and the valet in black seems like nothing more than a bit of editorializing on the director's part. The vital thing about this film, however, is its overall dazzling effect and its faithfulness to Mozart as well.

Filmed in and around Vicenza, near Venice, the action opens in a glass factory, amid smoke and flames. Throughout, this film is a feast for the eyes—there are scenes of rolling hills, boats on silvery canals, mysterious alleyways, sinister graveyards, and the opulent furnishings of the Don's mansion. Both Raimondi and Te Kanawa were in their first full bloom in 1978, and these roles are arguably their finest. This tends to be a dark, humorless *Don Giovanni*—a valid interpretation. Raimondi's Don (at Losey's direction, surely) is defiant, cynical, and virile, and Te Kanawa's Donna Elvira, in addition to being perfectly sung, is a good portrait of an innocent gone wrong.

Edda Moser is a spirited, furious, tonally accurate Donna Anna, with only a tendency to sharp during exclamatory passages marring her work. Kenneth Riegel's somewhat tight tenor is intelligently used, and "Il mio tesoro" is nicely sung. Teresa Berganza plays Zerlina as a lusty wench, and her insinuating mezzo sounds well placed. Her Masetto is Malcolm King, a good singer who is often overlooked, particularly in this part.

José Van Dam, one of the world's greatest singing actors, conveys Leporello's duplicity from the start and sings with such lush tone that he sounds at times like Raimondi (which makes the second-act role-switching scene even more effective). John Macurdy growls away as the Commendatore (and gets some of the words wrong) but makes his point.

It is doubtful whether the Paris Opera orchestra has ever sounded better. Maazel's tempi, on the quick side, carry the drama to its inevitable grim conclusion. In short, this is a necessary *Don Giovanni*—a pleasure to see and hear.

■ Tchaikovsky: *Eugene Onegin*

Galina Vishnevskaya, Anton Gregoriev, Yevgeny Kibkalo, Ivan Petrov, soloists; Orchestra and Chorus of the Bolshoi Theatre, Boris Khaikin, cond.

Corinth Video, color, 1958, 106 minutes. Russian with English subtitles.

This is an odd entry in the *Onegin* sweepstakes: a filmed abridgment of the opera in which actors lip-synch the voices of the singers noted above. As such, it is in a category all its own, but on its own terms it is highly successful. Director Roman Tikhomirov uses the camera wisely and fully exploits the medium—in the letter scene Tatiana verbalizes about half the text; the rest is in her mind, and we even get to see Onegin reading her letter.

The colors are vivid and bright, and the accent is on realism, with wheat fields, arbors, ballrooms, deserted streets, and blue skies. The actors who lip-synch are excellent—youthful and involved—as is the singing. Vishnevskaya, in her early thirties in 1958, sings beautifully as Tatiana, and one wonders why she wasn't chosen to do her own acting as well. Anton Gregoriev is a lighter-voiced-than-usual Lensky; accordingly, the actor looks like a very young man. Ivan Petrov both sings and acts Gremin with authority.

Yevgeny Kibkalo sounds fresh and vibrant as Onegin, and Vadim Medvedev plays him as somewhat of a dandy. The remainder of the cast is up to par, and Boris Khaikin leads the Bolshoi forces energetically. The cuts are wisely chosen and comprise mostly repeats in ensembles and occasionally entire passages whose absence does not damage the story's continuity. In short, this is a wonderful film version of the opera, full of surprises and true to itself. The subtitles, by the way, are excellent.

■ Handel: *Julius Caesar*

Janet Baker, Valerie Masterson, Sarah Walker, Della Jones, James Bowman, John Tomlinson; English National Opera Orchestra and Chorus, Charles Mackerras, cond.

HBO Video, color, 1984, 179 minutes (two cassettes). English.

Handel's *Giulio Cesare* was first performed in 1724 with the great alto castrato, Senesino, as Cesare. In this 1984 studio performance, Janet Baker sings the title role, and her voice has a timbre close to Senesino's, adding a certain validity to the proceedings. Baker is, by turns, commanding, amorous, and subtle; the role's difficult coloratura holds no fears for her.

We get a full portrait of the lover-warrior Caesar, and it is a tribute to her acting ability that we never feel uncomfortable with her in this challenging trouser role.

Soprano Valerie Masterson is an alluring Cleopatra—only a Caesar made of stone could resist her. Her high-flying vocal line is secure and seems almost matter-of-fact. It's a fine performance. Mezzo-sopranos Sarah Walker and Della Jones, as the mother and son Cornelia and Sextus, move and sing equally well. Countertenor James Bowman as Ptolemy—once one accepts his hooting sound and vaguely clownlike costumes—is convincingly villainous.

Brian Trowell's excellent English translation and John Copley's direction help make the show dramatically convincing, while the sets and costumes, by John Pascoe and Michael Stennett respectively, are quite opulent and colorful. The inventive camerawork makes the rather stiff *da*

Valerie Masterson as Cleopatra in a scene from the English National Opera production of Handel's *Julius Caesar*. Courtesy HBO Video.

capo form of the arias flow smoothly. Conductor Charles Mackerras and the ENO forces cannot be praised enough. This performance isn't likely to be bettered—highly recommended.

■ Tippett: *King Priam*

Rodney Macann, Sarah Walker, Howard Haskin, Anne Mason, Janet Price, Neil Jenkins, Omar Ebrahim, other soloists; Kent Opera Orchestra and Chorus, Roger Norrington, cond. Directed by Nicholas Hytner; directed for television by Robin Lough.

Home Vision, color, 1985, 135 minutes. English.

King Priam is arguably Michael Tippett's masterpiece, and the Kent Opera has given it a beautiful production. The taping took place under studio conditions, permitting crosscutting and tricks with images that all add to the effect. Never a composer to deal with lighthearted subjects, Tippett had leaned heavily toward the metaphysical in *The Midsummer Marriage* and, later, in *The Knot Garden,* often distancing audiences with his obscure meanings. In *Priam* the subject is once again deeply serious—the inevitability of death—but this time the libretto and music are powerful and comprehensible.

The design by David Fielding is vaguely surreal, as is the opera, and so the white walls, bombed-out buildings, and slightly futuristic costumes pose no problems. They are part of the mood—bleak, stark, and true. Tippett occasionally uses a solo piano in the orchestra (reminiscent of Britten's *The Turn of the Screw*), while at other times he relies only on winds and occasionally scores for strings alone. This complicated work is a bit long and can't be called a grand old time for everyone. But those with a taste for contemporary opera or a curiosity as to what is going on in the modern operatic world should definitely take a look.

Rodney Macann is perfect as the doomed Priam, singing with flawless diction and a round, full tone and using his bass-baritone expressively. When he orders the murder of the baby Paris (because an old seer has foreseen Priam's death by Paris' hand), we know that he cannot stop or change the future—and he knows it, too. His wife, Hecuba, is sung by Janet Price, whose dramatic coloratura is well placed in this difficult and somewhat thankless role. She, too, knows doom when she sees it. The difficult role of Paris is sung by Howard Haskin, who is pushed a bit far.

Baritone Omar Ebrahim sings a passionate Hector. One of the work's high points comes at the end of the second act, when Hector, Paris, and Priam join in a trio of triumph as they smear their bodies with the blood of Patroclus. Achilles' Valkyrielike war cry is heard over their rejoicing, and his face, full of fury, is superimposed over theirs. Achilles, here played as a homosexual, is written for a heldentenor, and Neil Jenkins is superb. John Hancorn's Patroclus, too, is finely drawn.

Anne Mason's Helen of Troy is appropriately alluring, and Sarah Walker's Andromache is unforgettable—her moving lament at the start of the third act and her later confrontation with Helen are high points. The others in the cast are all up to their tasks, but special mention must be made of tenor Christopher Gillett, whose final-act monologue ties all the loose ends together.

This is a fascinating music drama, impeccably handled, even if deciding what is real and what is imagined is often left up to the viewer. Congratulations to all involved for bringing this rewarding work to vivid life.

■ *Laugh, Pagliacci*

Beniamino Gigli, Alida Valli, Mario Boriello; directed by Giuseppe Fatigati.

Lyric Distribution, black & white, 1947, 84 minutes. Italian with English subtitles.

The wonderful thing about this film and others like it is how seriously the performers take it. No matter how murky the plot, with flashbacks within flashbacks and characters who change character in midfilm, everyone remains sincere throughout, with the obvious hope of making us shed a tiny tear at its close. The story concerns Canio, the cuckold clown who killed his wife, Nedda, and her lover in *Pagliacci*. Let out of jail, Canio returns home, tells the local composer, Leoncavallo, his story, and tries to speak with the daughter he left behind. (She has been raised as an aristocrat and knows nothing of him or his murdering ways.) Gigli plays a tenor named Morelli for whom the opera is eventually composed. (Between scenes we get to see him in snippets from other operas.) Canio finally does get to speak with his daughter, but he denies that he's known her before—much to the relief of the other characters—and walks off into the distance to the strains of "Vesti la giubba." Fortunately, the subtitles are so often placed against a white background that they're unreadable, and if you don't speak or understand Italian you're better off inventing what's going on. Occasionally the subtitles just stop altogether—a real fringe benefit.

Gigli, never a great actor, doesn't have to act here, and his voice is at its most meltingly lyrical. The film opens with his reading of the famous prologue from the opera (transposed up a semitone), and it's a stunner. Later we hear the whole tenor line from the duet "Prendi, l'anel ti dono" from Bellini's *La Sonnambula,* and it is doubtful that any tenor has ever sung it with such melting *mezza voce.* Thereafter we get enough of *Pagliacci* not to feel cheated, and Gigli sings with his usual passion, sobs, gleaming tone, and gentleness. All plot problems are forgiven once the singing begins. Would that there were more of it!

The role of the daughter is taken by the young, beautiful Alida Valli. Occasionally other characters sing, but they are invariably in the background. The picture is cloudy, but the sound is clear enough. This is a work for specialists interested in a certain type of film that was in vogue many years ago—and, of course, for Gigli fans.

■ Mozart: *The Magic Flute*

Soloists; the Swedish State Broadcasting Network Symphony, Eric Ericson, cond. Directed by Ingmar Bergman.

Paramount Home Video, color, 1973, 134 minutes. Swedish with English subtitles.

Despite everything, this performance is beyond reproach or criticism. It doesn't matter that the Swedish language does not trip off the tongue with Mozart's music, or that, apart from the Papageno of Jorma Hynninen, no member of the cast is vocally on an international level, or even that a few of them, the Queen of the Night in particular, actually make some rather unoperatic sounds. Nor does it matter that there are cuts and some rearranging of scenes. Every opera lover should have this performance, which is so full of wonder and enchantment that experiencing it is akin to hearing the *The Magic Flute* for the first time.

From the first bars of the overture, during which director Ingmar Bergman pans from face to face in the audience, we realize that we will be seeing more than just a staged movie of Mozart's masterpiece. And indeed, we get to see the singers backstage (in a replica of Sweden's perfectly preserved eighteenth-century Drottningholm Court Theatre), studying their scores (with Sarastro studying Wagner's *Parsifal* at one point), and preparing for their roles. By the time the opera is over, we understand the creative process better, feel much closer to the characters, and have a greater sense of what Mozart intended *The Magic Flute* to be.

The orchestral playing and the singing are rarely better than good, but it hardly matters. We come away with the spirit of the score, and few performances of this opera so fully achieve that goal. Don't miss this one.

■ Verdi: *Otello*

Placido Domingo, Katia Ricciarelli, Justino Diaz, Ezio DiCesare, other soloists; Orchestra and Chorus of La Scala, Milan, Lorin Maazel, cond. Directed by Franco Zeffirelli.

Kultur, color, 1985, 123 minutes. Italian with English subtitles.

Both opera lovers and movie lovers had reason to look forward to the release of this film, coming, as it did, on the heels of Zeffirelli's admirable *La Traviata*. Unfortunately, the results are at best controversial.

Billed as "Zeffirelli's *Otello*," the film is precisely that: a conflation of excerpts from what is arguably Verdi's greatest score. The director has not only cut almost thirty minutes of the original; his reinterpretations of the story are both ignorant and anti-Verdian, not to mention anti-Shakespearean. The rarely performed third-act ballet is here placed in the first act, the love duet is sung not on the ramparts but in the couple's bedroom, Desdemona is not slain in her bed, Otello kills Iago at the opera's close, and there are further errors in judgment. This is not a performance for purists or opera lovers.

However, the look of the production is almost worth the price of the tape; in this respect movie fans will not be disappointed. The locations are spectacular, as are the costumes and the scenery, and the casting has been done with an eye toward cinematic realism.

All three principals look and act their parts wonderfully, and the role of Cassio is nicely sung by Ezio DiCesare and well acted by someone else. Domingo is *the* Otello for our age, secure at both ends of his range, and his portrayal of the Moor is moving, though his performance is sabotaged by the many cuts. Ricciarelli is in fine vocal form and looks radiant, causing concern only when she puts undue pressure on her voice. It would have been nice to hear her "Willow Song," but it, too, is cut. Justino Diaz gets through the role of Iago with swagger and great credibility, but one senses that he was helped vocally by the engineers. Lorin Maazel favors generally slow tempi, and the La Scala forces are magnificent. The sound is sometimes too loud, the noise of the storm all but overwhelming Verdi's opening first chord.

In the end, this film is a great opportunity lost. It is recommended only for film enthusiasts and for those opera lovers with a high tolerance for Zeffirellian blasphemy.

■ Verdi: *Otello*

Mario del Monaco, Rosanna Carteri, Renato Capecchi, Plinio Clabassi, other soloists; Orchestra and Chorus of RAI, Tullio Serafin, cond.

Lyric Distribution, black & white, 1958, 136 minutes. Italian, no subtitles.

This film was apparently made for Italian TV, since the sound track was prerecorded and the singers lip-synch. One ostensible reason for making it was that Mario del Monaco was the preeminent Otello of his day and was a matinee idol in his native land. He is in spectacular, steely voice here, and were we not living in the time of Vickers and Domingo (whose portrayals have more introspection and depth), del Monaco's performance would be easier to like. His is a purely vocal performance, emphasizing lung power and little else, but it cannot be dismissed. No dramatic tenor has come along with this type of sound since, and as a memento of another era, it is worth hearing.

Rosanna Carteri is a lovely Desdemona, singing with a light, sweet tone and reaching emotional and lyrical heights in her extended final-act scena. Renato Capecchi is a snarling, mean Iago, and bass Plinio Clabassi adds a bit of class to the minor part of Lodovico. Tullio Serafin was a master conductor, and the entire performance holds together and moves along superbly.

The picture quality is unremittingly dark to the point of obscuring the action, and the director's insistence on close-ups makes for uncomfortable viewing. This film is an interesting museum piece but, in the end, delivers less than it promises. Del Monaco fans may want to own this, but because of the terrible quality of the film itself, few others will want to make the investment.

■ Leoncavallo: *Pagliacci*

Richard Tauber, Steffi Duna, Diana Napier, Arthur Margetson, Esmond Knight, others; conducted by Albert Coates.

Lyric Distribution, black & white, 1937, 80 minutes. English.

This ancient film is so bizarre that it is actually appealing. In this version Leoncavallo's music and plot are completely rearranged: Silvio is in the army, Tonio has a girlfriend, the entire cast gets caught in a blizzard, and the characters talk nonsense.

The main reason to see this tape is Richard Tauber, whose great tenor voice is heard to remarkable advantage here. Never mind that everyone else speaks with a British accent—when Tauber sings we forgive all. He sings the prologue (normally sung by the baritone) up a semitone, and very movingly. He sings Silvio's part of the duet, some of the chorus's music, Beppe's aria (from the play scene), and most of Canio's music. Tauber was a classic and classy tenor, and he sings here with a long, pure line and a handsome, full tone.

The quality of the picture, unfortunately, is vintage 1937, and so is the sound. The conductor is the great, underrated Wagnerian, Albert Coates, but his presence doesn't really count for the purposes of this film.

■ Tchaikovsky: *Pique Dame*

Tamara Milashkina, Larisa Avdeyeva, Sofia Preobrazhenskaya, Zurab Andzhaparidze, Yevgeny Kibkalo, V. Nechipailo, soloists; Orchestra and Chorus of the Bolshoi Theatre, Yevgeny Svetlanov, cond.

Corinth Films, 1960, color, 102 minutes. Russian with English subtitles.

This is an abridgment of Tchaikovsky's sinister opera *Pique Dame*, with actors lip-synching roles sung by well-known members of the Bolshoi Opera. Almost an hour of the work has been cut, mostly comprising the dance and choral sequences; but the riveting drama itself, based on a poem by Pushkin, remains intact, and this tale of a gambling soldier's descent into madness comes across vividly.

Much of the credit must go to director Roman Tikhomirov, who keeps the action at a fast pace, concentrating on the plot's grimmer, frightening aspects. The scene in which the soldier, Herman (well sung by tenor And-zhaparidze and acted by O. Strizhenov), scares the old countess (eerily sung by Sofia Preobrazhenskaya) literally to death is unforgettable. Soprano Tamara Milashkina is an exquisitely fragile Lisa, and V. Nechi-pailo makes the most of the role of Tomsky.

The color is almost too sharp, but the sound is good. Aside from some awkward lip-synching and the fact that this *is* an abridgment, this superb film can be wholeheartedly recommended. Overall, it is a most effective retelling of the opera.

■ Borodin: *Prince Igor*

V. Kinayev, Tamara Milashkina, I. Noreika, V. Malyshev, Yev-geny Nesterenko; Ballet, Orchestra and Chorus of the Kirov The-atre, Gennady Provatorov, cond. Directed by Roman Tikhomirov.

Corinth Video, color, 1969, 105 minutes. Russian with English subtitles.

This is a movie version of a bit more than half of Borodin's opera *Prince Igor*. The work was left unfinished at the composer's death; it was com-pleted, orchestrated, and rearranged by Alexander Glazunov and Rimsky-Korsakov. In most performances of the work the third act is left out, as it is in this film, except for an energetic tenor-bass duet. This is an opera about which arguments rage as to which scenes to include, which to shorten, and so on. Since this is the only tape of *Prince Igor* that we're likely to have for some time, we're lucky that it's as good as it is, even if it is shortened.

Filmed in lush color with many outdoor shots of the steppes and other imaginative cinematic touches (some arias are performed as interior mono-logues), the people we see are not the ones we hear. The actors ride horses, get caught in downpours, run and hide, all the while lip-synching their musical lines. It somehow works, even if the whole affair has a flashy, spaghetti Western look to it. Director Roman Tikhomirov has cho-sen native locales and able actors, and the somewhat confused drama comes to life, probably making more of an effect than it might on stage. (Staged performances of the work are rare in the West.) Bass Yevgeny Nesterenko as Konchak and soprano Tamara Milashkina as Yaroslavna are the only two names some Westerners will recognize. V. Kinayev in the title role is also impressive.

This is clearly a film for special tastes, but it does give us a glimpse of a certain long-gone type of filmmaking and performance style that still has its fascination.

■ Verdi: *Rigoletto*

Tito Gobbi, Mario Filippeschi, Lina Pagliughi, Giulio Neri, soloists; orchestra and chorus conducted by Tullio Serafin.

Lyric Distribution, black & white, 1947, 97 minutes. Italian, no subtitles.

Gobbi and Serafin are reason enough to own this tape. Their performances are reminders of what is currently rare on the operatic scene: the true Verdian style. Gobbi was at the start of his international career here, and while he clearly never possessed the lushest of voices, his Rigoletto fairly leaps off the screen. He is alternately sneering and contemptuous at court, and loving and protective at home. His is a moving, believable performance.

Mario Filippeschi's Duke is stylish, if a bit dull. Lina Pagliughi's Gilda (the role is played in the film by a prettier, thinner, but not much better actress) is charming and a touch shallow. The black-voiced bass Giulio Neri as Sparafucile is a bonus and brings real menace to the role. The rest of the cast is excellent, and the chorus and the unnamed orchestra play stunningly for Serafin.

The picture quality is acceptable, but there may be a problem with the sound. The review copy was close to a semitone sharp, and picky buyers with sensitive ears might want to check it out before investing. If all's well, don't miss this one.

■ Strauss: *Der Rosenkavalier*

Sena Jurinac, Elisabeth Schwarzkopf, Anneliese Rothenberger, Otto Edelmann, Erich Kunz; Vienna State Opera Chorus, Vienna Philharmonic Orchestra, Mozarteum Orchestra, Herbert von Karajan, cond. Produced and directed by Paul Czinner.

VAI, color, 1962, 190 minutes (two cassettes). German, no subtitles.

Upon its release, this film was instantly proclaimed a classic, and it is easy to see why. All of the singers are in top voice, von Karajan conducts brilliantly but has not yet developed the eccentricities that later crept into his operatic readings, the sets and costumes are lush, and the direction is superlative. And of course, there's the Marschallin of Elisabeth Schwarzkopf, which many consider definitive. Certainly, few singers, if any, have come closer to the heart of this complex character.

The main problem with her characterization is that every moment, every phrase, every movement seem to have been planned in advance. She coos, she cajoles, she carries herself with exquisite dignity and grace, but it's all too perfect. Some will have no complaints; others will fault this lack of spontaneity, the calculated edge to all her actions. But there's no denying that the voice is shimmering silver and that she is a beautiful Marschallin. One might just prefer more—for want of a better word—soul.

If this criticism seems harsh one need only compare Schwarzkopf's performance with that of her Octavian, Sena Jurinac, who is the picture of naturalness; every move comes straight from the character. It's studied, but the seams are invisible, and though her voice lacks some depth, her portrayal is flawless.

Otto Edelmann sings Baron Ochs smoothly from top to bottom and paints the perfect picture of a boor. His lecherous smirking and attitude of noblesse oblige are properly annoying, and Schwarzkopf has just the right reactions of delicate disgust for him. Anneliese Rothenberger as Sophie sings beautifully although she looks too much like a Kewpie doll in the second act. Erich Kunz is Faninal, and he gets into the heart of this character, who can take just so much before he explodes. Giuseppe Zampieri is the Italian tenor, singing his own aria with gleaming tone. The rest of the cast is ideal.

Von Karajan leads the orchestras and chorus in this Salzburg Festival production masterfully, although one could wish he had given the third-act trio more room to unfold. The camerawork is for the most part excellent, although there is some sloppy editing.

No matter how one feels about Schwarzkopf's Marschallin, it is impossible not to respect her portrayal and use it as a benchmark for others. This pair of cassettes should be in every serious opera lover's collection.

■ Verdi: *La Traviata*

Teresa Stratas, Placido Domingo, Cornell MacNeil, Allan Monk; Orchestra and Chorus of the Metropolitan Opera, James Levine, cond. Directed by Franco Zeffirelli.

MCA Home Video, color, 1982, 105 minutes. Italian with English subtitles.

This film is proof that Zeffirelli *can* turn out the ultimate opera film, using all of the most modern techniques, and still remain faithful to the music. Here he uses flashbacks, double exposures, quick cuts, filtered shots, and out-of-focus and mood shots to enhance this production. As usual, he overdoes it. The staging is too lavish, there are too many flashbacks (and flashbacks within flashbacks), and he takes a few liberties with the score. Still, this is a great *Traviata*—the first two acts are movingly romantic, the party scenes are manic and fun, and the intimate moments truthful and touching.

Oddly, not until one has become thoroughly familiar with this film (which was first released in theatres) does one realize how mediocre some of the singing is, and how little it matters. Stratas is in poor voice in the first act, and "Sempre libera" is transposed down a semitone for her. But she is a most touching Violetta—by turns rough, soft, angry, bruised, overwhelmed, helpless, hopeless—and beautiful throughout. Domingo, too, is not totally comfortable with the role of Alfredo, but his gambling scene is powerful, and he is tender and gentle in the final act. Cornell MacNeil's Germont is a bore; though he is in fine voice, he fails to make much of an impression. Allan Monk makes more of Douphol than usual, and the rest of the cast is excellent. Zeffirelli manages to give each "extra" an individual personality, and the typecasting is just right.

James Levine, billed as both conductor and "musical director" (one assumes he chose the cuts together with the director), leans toward quick tempi, but this only backfires in "Dite alla giovane" and in Violetta's repeated utterances at the start of the gambling scene. The Met's chorus and orchestra are at their considerable best.

This film is an imaginative and successful merging of two art forms, cinematic tricks and all. One can disagree with Zeffirelli's editorializing, but his musical understanding and dramatic vision are beyond reproach.

■ Rimsky-Korsakov: *The Tsar's Bride*

Galina Vishnevskaya, Larisa Avdeyeva, T. Kibkalo, V. Nuzhny, others; the Bolshoi Opera, Yevgeny Svetlanov, cond.

Corinth Films, black & white, 1963, 95 minutes. Russian with English subtitles.

This very successful abridgment (about one hour of the music has been cut) of Rimsky-Korsakov's 1899 masterpiece is the only available performance on either disc or tape, and so it is recommended if for no other reason. The confusing plot concerns Marfa, who is in love with Ivan but is adored by Gryaznoy, whose mistress, Lyubasha, therefore poisons her. After drinking the poison (Gryaznoy believes it to be the love potion he bought to seduce her, but Lyubasha substituted poison at the last moment), Marfa in the third act is chosen to be the bride of Ivan the Terrible. In the final act, just about everyone dies.

The film, in correctly austere black-and-white, features fine actors lip-synching some of the greatest voices of the Bolshoi Opera. (The only exception is Nuzhny, who both sings and acts the role of Ivan.) Undoubtedly the vocal star is Galina Vishnevskaya as Marfa, who sings with great expressivity and beauty. Larisa Avdeyeva sings the evil Lyubasha so as to make us understand her love for Gryaznoy (the actress is equally good) and sympathize with her. Nuzhny's Ivan is a bit strident, but Kibkalo makes Gryaznoy's music come to life.

This is an odd but highly interesting operatic experience. The Bolshoi forces are first-rate, Svetlanov conducts with authority, and the subtitles are clear. Perhaps the opera will come back into favor (the Washington Opera staged it in 1986). It's well worth seeing and hearing.

■ Puccini: *Turandot*

Lucille Udovick, Renata Mattioli, Franco Corelli, Mario Borriello, Mario Carlin, Renato Ercolani, Plinio Clabassi, soloists; Orchestra and Chorus of RAI Milan, Fernando Previtali, cond.

Legato Publishing Co., black & white, 1961, 115 minutes. Italian, no subtitles.

The main interest in this Italian film of a staged, lip-synched *Turandot* dating from the early 1960s is the presence of Franco Corelli as Calaf, the unknown prince. Corelli was the perfect *tenore di forza*, with a rich, full bottom range and bright, ringing top notes, and with a flawless register in between. He was a natural for Calaf, and this film catches him at his best.

Little-known American soprano Lucille Udovick sings the title role. Based on this portrayal, she was a singer of substantial voice if not much shading, and her Turandot is good though not great. Renata Mattioli is a sweet if unexceptional Liù, and bass Plinio Clabassi makes an unusually moving Timur. Borriello, Carlin, and Ercolani sing beautifully but act clownishly as Ping, Pang, and Pong, and both orchestra and chorus perform well under Fernando Previtali's well-schooled, urgent baton.

There are some nice cinematic effects when Turandot appears in the first act, and the picture is a very acceptable black-and-white. This video is recommended if only for Corelli. We haven't heard a Calaf like his since the 1960s.

■ Massenet: *Werther*

Peter Dvorsky, Brigitte Fassbaender, Magdalena Vasary, Hans Helm; orchestra conducted by Libor Pešek. Directed by Peter Weigl.

European Video Distributors, color, 1985, 107 minutes. French, no subtitles.

This film, a coproduction of West German and Czech television, is a good-looking, fine-sounding version of Massenet's sentimental masterpiece. All of the choral music and recitatives have been cut, leaving us, in effect, with what *Werther* actually is—an extended love duet. The "local color" episodes apparently are used as a way of dispelling the intensity of young Werther's gloom.

The outdoor scenes, filled with ladies in large hats and lovely costumes, evoke the correct mood from the start. Director Peter Weigl moves the action along, but his singers aren't always up to the physical demands of the acting. In fact, aside from Peter Dvorsky's Werther and Brigitte Fassbaender's Charlotte, the roles are sung by one person and lip-synched and acted by another—sometimes very poorly. Hans Helm, as Albert, Charlotte's husband, sounds mature but the role is played by a young man; Magdalena Vasary's Sophie is prettily sung but badly acted by someone older than the part requires.

The two leads, however, are rather good. Peter Dvorsky, an excellent Czech tenor, unfortunately lacks a distinctive sound. The voice is rock-solid and bright, but he tends not to vary his vocal colors and to under-interpret, and his acting is a bit monochromatic. Yet, oddly enough, his portrayal of the title character is a success.

Fassbaender is an important mezzo-soprano, with a bright sound and a good sense of drama, and her acting is as impressive as her singing. Her third-act letter scene is genuinely touching (some viewers will mourn the lack of subtitles here), and she never makes an unattractive sound.

The color is a bit washed out; perhaps this is the director's way of editorializing. (There's a wonderful opening scene in which Werther sings about nature and the camera gives us his skewed vision of the world.) In summation, not the ultimate *Werther* but a credible, interesting film that, for all its faults, serves the work well.

Opera: Concerts and Recitals

■ Maria Callas: Hamburg Concert, May 15, 1959

Arias from *La Vestale* (Spontini), *Macbeth* (Verdi), *Il Barbiere di Siviglia* (Rossini), *Don Carlo* (Verdi), *Il Pirata* (Bellini). Maria Callas, soprano, Orchestra of Süddeutscher Rundfunk, Nicola Rescigno, cond.

Kultur, black & white, 68 minutes. Italian, no subtitles.

■ Maria Callas: Hamburg Concert, March 16, 1962

Arias from *Le Cid* (Massenet), *Carmen* (Bizet), *Ernani* (Verdi), *La Cenerentola* (Rossini), *Don Carlo* (Verdi); orchestral excerpts by Bizet and Berlioz. Maria Callas, soprano, Orchestra of Norddeutscher Rundfunk, Georges Prêtre, cond.

Kultur, black & white, 66 minutes. French and Italian, no subtitles.

To say that Maria Callas changed the way we listen to opera in the second half of the twentieth century is a statement with which few would argue; to explain precisely how she did this is a bit more controversial. Unfortunately, with the exception of her sad and ill-advised comeback tour with Giuseppe di Stefano in the early 1970s, Callas stopped singing in public a quarter century ago, so an entire generation of operagoers has never seen her. These two cassettes will be a spectacular eye-opener for them—and everyone else.

The 1959 concert finds Callas in very fresh voice; she had not sung for almost two months. It comprises arias from operas that she had sung onstage although, in some cases, infrequently and many years before. During this period, Callas was having great difficulties with her high C;

she avoids the note entirely at the close of both the Spontini and Bellini selections. Her reading of the former is full of urgency and pleading, and the middle of the voice is rich and full. Callas turns the *Pirata* finale into a miniopera: looking ravishing, her huge eyes filled with confusion and her long fingers grasping and searching, her acting alone during the orchestral prelude stands as a lesson to aspiring singers and actresses. Happily, the lengthy scene itself is superbly sung, with perfectly articulated runs and a legato line that defines the word. The top C is missed at the scene's close. It's needed here, and the G is an anticlimax.

Both Verdi arias are models of style: the Lady Macbeth is demonic (though with some pretty wiry top notes), the Elisabetta, regal. "Tu che le vanità" is given a spacious, noble reading, and the voice is secure. The Rossini aria was a specialty of Callas's, and although her sound was, arguably, not suited to comedy, she does Rosina full justice and the coloratura is managed with ease, grace, and spirit. Nicola Rescigno and the orchestra offer fine support throughout.

The 1962 concert comprises arias that Callas never sang in context, all but one of which was composed with the mezzo-soprano range in mind. Again, one is amazed at how quickly and completely she captures a character. Callas begins with a deeply felt "Pleurez, mes yeux" and then changes gears for the two excerpts from Carmen. She *is* the coquettish, dangerous gypsy, and the voice, under some pressure throughout this recital, is comfortable in this music. The *Ernani* aria, shorn of its cabaletta, is a bit rushed but is still a nice, moody reading.

The real joys of this tape, however, are the *Cenerentola* and *Don Carlo* arias. The former is light and sincere, although the high B at its close is unfortunate. Eboli's aria is a full portrait, filled with self-loathing, sorrow, and finally hope, and the singing has terrific urgency.

The orchestra (which also plays Berlioz' Roman Carnival Overture and the preludes from the first and third acts of *Carmen*) plays well, and with the exception of the *Ernani* miscalculation, Georges Prêtre paces sensibly. Both the picture and sound throughout are better than we had any reason to hope for.

These cassettes are not only historical documents but also entertaining and enlightening additions to any collection.

■ *José Carreras in Concert*

José Carreras, tenor; Vincenzo Scalera, piano. Recorded live, Komische Oper, East Berlin, January 9, 1987.

Kultur, color, 1987, 90 minutes.

This concert was taped about six months before Catalan tenor José Carreras was discovered to have leukemia. He looks his best and sings with exquisite tone but occasionally forces the voice unpleasantly. His innate musicality and emotional involvement remain a joy to hear, even if the high A and B-flat at *forte* have a distinct beat. Carreras can indeed sing these notes softly if he chooses, and no other reigning tenor can claim that.

The program is generous. Four beautiful songs by Paolo Tosti open the recital (only three are listed on the cassette box). Outstanding are "Vorrei morire" for Carreras' lovely *pianissimo* singing and sensitive phrasing, and the dark sound he brings to "L'ultima canzone." Songs by Bellini, Denza, Leoncavallo, and Respighi follow, and they're all well served, although Respighi's "Nebbie" lacks the ultimate feeling of bleakness that it requires to be totally effective.

The four Spanish songs are the perfect measure of this tenor's art. The Ginastera is more conventionally appealing than one might guess, Carlos Guastavino's "La Rosa y el sauce" is lovely, Ernesto Halffter's "Fado" ends on a perfectly whispered high A-flat, and Sorozabal's "No puede ser" is performed more introspectively than usual. (Compare it with Domingo's thrilling, if slightly too *macho* performance on Kultur's "An Evening with Placido Domingo.") The four rarely-performed Puccini songs that end the printed program are a revelation. "Sole e amore" contains the same melody that appears in *La Bohème*'s third act, and the highly dramatic and exclamatory "Mentia l'avviso" is apparently a sketch for Des Grieux' "Donna non vidi mai" from *Manon Lescaut*.

There are six encores. In Cardillo's "Cor 'ngrato," the ultimate Neapolitan song, Carreras shows that he can pull out all the stops when the music asks for it. Next comes the stunning "Lamento di Federico" from Cilea's *L'Arlesiana*; the tenor brings just the right combination of ringing tone and *morbidezza* (delicacy) to it. The rendition of "Granada" is stirring without ever being vulgar, and Leonard Bernstein's "Tonight" from *West Side Story* is passionately sung though Carreras is obviously a bit tired. A song by Rodolfo Falvo calms the crowd a bit, but "Nessun dorma" from Puccini's *Turandot*, transposed down a semitone, brings it to its feet. The tenor remains reserved, and it is amazing how little he tries to ingratiate himself with the audience. He serves the music well at all times, using his burnished tone and occasionally frayed voice as a means of intense communication. His concentration is extraordinary. Vincenzo Scalera, his accompanist, is considerate, intelligent, and respectful of the music and the performer. Highly recommended.

■ An Evening with Placido Domingo

Placido Domingo, Martha Senn, Edouard Tumagian; English Chamber Orchestra, Eugene Kohn, cond.

Kultur, color, 1987, 55 minutes.

This benefit concert was given on June 21, 1987, at London's Wembley Stadium, for the victims of Mexico City's 1985 earthquake. It is appropriately showy considering the venue, though bathing the tenor in blue light at various times during the evening does give the impression that the next stop is Las Vegas. Happily, however, the music and its presentation overshadow any reservations about the setting. Domingo exudes his usual charm and is in remarkable voice.

Domingo opens with the brief and beautiful "Amor ti vieta" from Giordano's *Fedora*—always a good idea, as it sits comfortably for his voice and its lovely melodic line draws the audience in. Although Domingo has sung "Ch'ella mi creda" from *La Fanciulla del West* dozens of times, it seems fresh and new here. Mezzo-soprano Martha Senn then joins Domingo for the second-act duet from *Il Trovatore*, and while the tenor seems to be working too hard, the mezzo impresses with her full tone and dramatic commitment. The Romanian baritone Edouard Tumagian, who sings the fourth-act Marcello-Rodolfo duet from *Bohème* with the tenor, exhibits a handsome, shiny tone, a comfortable stage presence, and fine musicianship. He brings out the most poetic in Domingo, who softens his tone and delivery nicely for this sweet, sentimental duet.

After a brief introductory speech Domingo sings "On the Street Where You Live" from *My Fair Lady*. Halfway through he charmingly apologizes for his heavily accented English and finishes the song in Spanish. An aria from *The Merry Widow*, in Spanish, is followed by a very effective zarzuela aria and duet, the latter again with Senn, and a highly melodramatic rendition of Sorozabal's "No puede ser" (compare it with Carreras' version, also available on Kultur). Domingo offers two encores: the Neapolitan song "Cor 'ngrata," which he sings with passion, and the ever popular "Granada."

There are moments when Domingo sounds not only more beautiful but more interesting than ever, and his evident happiness onstage infects everyone. Granted, the same arm movements over and over are a bit tedious, but if one can cope with Pavarotti's handkerchief, one can cope with anything. This is a perfect hour's entertainment and is recommended highly.

■ *Sherrill Milnes: An All-Star Gala*

Sherrill Milnes, Julia Migenes-Johnson, Mirella Freni, Peter Schreier, Placido Domingo; the London Symphony Orchestra, Anton Guadagno, cond; the Staatskapelle Berlin, Siegfried Kurz, Gunter Joseck, Sherrill Milnes, conductors.

VAI, color, 1985, 56 minutes.

Placido Domingo and Sherrill Milnes in the act-one duet from Verdi's *Don Carlo* as performed in *Sherrill Milnes: An All-Star Gala.* Courtesy Video Artists International.

There is about forty-five minutes of fine singing on this cassette. The remaining eleven minutes consist of Burt Lancaster chatting with us from, of all places, a carousel. Ignore it and go straight to the singing.

Milnes was in peak form for this taping, and he talks as well as he sings. The prologue from *Pagliacci* is performed with a storyteller's ear and a great baritone's voice, followed by a sweet duet from Sigmund Romberg's *Up in Central Park* in which the baritone is joined by the attractive and vocally pure Julia Migenes-Johnson. Both singers have the right, light style for the music.

Milnes then conducts Peter Schreier in an aria from *Così fan tutte*, and while the tenor sings wonderfully, one does have reservations about Milnes's conducting abilities. Brahms's "O Tod" finds Milnes out of his emotional depth, but the second-act duet from *La Traviata*, in which he is joined by the radiant Mirella Freni, is simple, direct, and very touching. Milnes and Domingo join for a ringing friendship duet from *Don Carlo*, and the baritone closes the program with an exciting "Credo" from *Otello*.

A successful evening's entertainment, then, but we could have done without the glitz and the chatter. One more caveat: most of the selections are lip-synched, and this could prove annoying for some people.

■ *Operafest: A Gala Concert at the Zurich Opera*

Excerpts from works by Wagner, Offenbach, Gounod, Donizetti, Verdi, Bizet, Rossini, Dvořák, Stravinsky, Tchaikovsky, Mozart, Strauss; with Gwyneth Jones, Alfredo Kraus, Sona Ghazarian, Thomas Hampson, Gunther Von Kannen, Mara Zampieri, Doris Soffel, José Carreras, Robert Hale, Nicolai Ghiaurov, Lucia Popp, Mirella Freni, Dorothea Wirtz, Christian Boesch, soloists; the Children's Chorus, Chorus, Orchestra, and Corps de Ballet of the Zurich Opera, Ferdinand Leitner, Ralf Weikert, André Presser, conductors.

VAI, color, 1986, 92 minutes.

This is an uneven offering, but it adds up to an enjoyable evening. Most of the applause has been eliminated so this is nonstop music; you may want to take a fifteen-minute break somewhere in the middle. The program opens with Gwyneth Jones's wobbly but exciting "Dich, teure Halle" from Wagner's *Tannhäuser* and continues with Alfredo Kraus and the men's chorus performing the ballad of Kleinzach (with a spectacular interpolated high C) from *The Tales of Hoffmann*.

Sona Ghazarian offers a pretty "Jewel Song" from *Faust*, and Gunther Von Kannen and the superb Thomas Hampson, in costume, race happily through the duet from *Don Pasquale*'s final act. The odd-voiced Mara Zampieri sails through an aria from *Un Ballo in Maschera*, and Carreras and Soffel nearly bring down the house with the final scene from *Carmen* in a staging of Jean-Pierre Ponnelle's peculiar production of that work.

Nicolai Ghiaurov then sings, quite beautifully, Don Basilio's aria from *Barber of Seville*. He is followed by the exquisite Lucia Popp, who sings "O Lovely Moon" (in Czech) from *Rusalka*, to absolute perfection. A brief excerpt from Balanchine's setting of the Stravinsky Violin Concerto shows off the company's corps de ballet nicely. Mirella Freni turns Tatiana's letter scene into a deeply moving mini-opera, and Christian Boesch and Dorothea Wirtz give a fine performance as Papageno and Papagena. At the show's close, the artists join in singing "Brüderlein" from *Die Fledermaus*.

This is a tape bursting with music—a nice potpourri.

■ *Pavarotti in London*

Luciano Pavarotti; Royal Philharmonic Orchestra, Kurt Herbert Adler, cond.

RCA/Columbia Pictures Home Video, color, 1982, 78 minutes.

This concert, by the tenor who is arguably the world's most popular, was taped in London's Royal Albert Hall on April 13, 1982, in the presence of Elizabeth, the queen mother. It finds Pavarotti in superb voice and singing with his usual warmth and effervescence. The attendance of royalty, however, does not stop Pavarotti from offering an oddly skimpy program of only ten selections—the remainder of the evening is taken up with lengthy orchestral excerpts.

Nevertheless, one doesn't feel cheated by the brevity of his program. The two tenor arias from *Tosca* are sung with ravishing purity of line and exquisite control, "Lamento di Federico" and "Una furtiva lagrima" are models of tenderness and taste, and both the tomb aria from *Lucia di Lammermoor* and Macduff's aria from Verdi's *Macbeth* have precisely the right manly timbre. Both encores, "Nessun dorma" from Puccini's *Turandot* and Ernesto de Curtis' perennial bonbon "Torna a Surriento," bring the audience to its feet, roaring with approval.

His voice, always full of sunshine, has it here in abundance, and the tone is open and free throughout. Pavarotti has often been accused of skimming the surface of roles, but in concert, where beauty of sound is paramount, it matters less. Highly recommended.

■ *Renata Scotto: Prima Donna in Recital*

Renata Scotto, soprano; Thomas Fulton, pianist.

VAI, color, 1984, 99 minutes.

This recital is not for those who are unfamiliar with Scotto's art and voice. Taped in Tokyo in September 1984, it is a generous evening of songs and arias that span two hundred years of musical history. Sadly, it finds the soprano far from her best. Her usual musical insights and dramatic nuances are in abundance, but her sound is at times painful to listen to. In fact, the viewer-listener is rarely comfortable during the entire program.

The program opens with Handel's beautiful "Lascia ch'io piango," a

Renata Scotto with accompanist Thomas Fulton at NHK Auditorium, Tokyo, September, 1984. Courtesy Video Artists International.

work of extreme introspection and mellowness, but any sound above *pianissimo* finds Scotto's tone under pressure and far from alluring. Similarly, although two songs by Scarlatti are sung with the utmost delicacy, danger seems to lurk a note higher or a decibel louder. Verdi's "Stornello" is lively and deliciously sung, since rarely is a note sustained here, but "Tu che le vanità" from *Don Carlo*, while very slow and superbly drawn, is a chore to sit through.

Two Liszt and Respighi songs are successfully rendered, displaying Scotto's remarkable concentration on both words and music. With the many selections from Puccini—arias from *Edgar*, *Tosca*, and *Madama Butterfly*—the vocal problems are even more evident, but then so is the singer's great ability to communicate.

Thomas Fulton is everything an accompanist should be and more, but this recital is problematic. Fans of Renata Scotto may want to own it; others may find it too distressing.

■ *Joan Sutherland in Concert*

Songs and arias by Rossini, Handel, Tosti, Donizetti, Meyerbeer, Dvořák, Verdi, Rimsky-Korsakov; folk songs; Richard Bonynge, piano.

Kultur, color, 1982, 49 minutes.

This program was taped for TV in Perth, Australia, in 1982. For the most part, it offers a good idea of what has always been right and not so right with this great soprano.

The selections from *Alcina*, *Semiramide*, *Les Huguenots*, and *La Traviata* are all performed with the soprano's usual expertise, and with added sensitivity in the "Addio del passato" and a bit less fluidity in the "Bel raggio." The rarely performed "A mezzanotte" by Donizetti and Rossini's "Chanson de Zora" and "La Petite Bohémienne" are sung expressively and with a fine sense of their direct, clear line. Tosti's "Serenata" is given a dazzling reading, with new and welcome embellishments.

On the minus side are "Bonnie Marie of Argyle" and "Songs My Mother Taught Me," which need a purity of tone that a voice the size of Sutherland's cannot muster, no matter how great her art. Similarly, the touching "There's No Place Like Home" suffers because of poor diction; no more than five or six words at a stretch can be understood. Many Sutherland fans will want to own this tape. They won't be surprised or disappointed.

Opera:
Documentaries

■ **Monserrat Caballé:** *The Woman, the Diva*

Directed by Antonio Chic, staged by Joseph Wishy, produced by
TVE (TV Spain & Recisa). Selections from *Giulio Cesare, Adriana
Lecouvreur, La Bohème, La Forza del Destino, Mefistofele;* zarzuelas
and Spanish songs.

Kultur, color, 1983, 67 minutes.

A personal greeting in words and music from the great Spanish diva,
this program consists largely of Italian arias and Spanish songs presented
in a variety of settings. In between, Caballé introduces each number and
tells us how it relates to her both as a Spanish woman and as an artist.

This duality is not always clear, and the staginess occasionally
obtrudes. She performs Cleopatra's aria from Handel's *Giulio Cesare* without explaining how this wonderfully sung piece relates to her. Similarly,
the inclusion of some other arias is justified only on the grounds that they
come from operas whose locale is Spain. "Tu che le vanità" from *Don
Carlo* is sung in the monastery to which King Philip II actually retired;
"Pace, pace, mio Dio" is sung as she wanders dangerously close to the
edge of a precipice high in the Spanish hills.

Between operatic arias Caballé interpolates zarzuela numbers and
songs. Caballé is clearly a world-class singer—perhaps one of the last
genuine divas, and the voice is always in good form, even occasionally
inspired. But where is Caballé the woman? We see nothing of her husband, tenor Bernabé Marti, or any of her children.

Perhaps the most interesting aspect of this hour's medley of song is her demonstration of how she actually sings. Her jaw seems always free and relaxed, and while she takes enormous breaths to sustain some of her phrasing, she never appears to labor. Many segments are lip-synched, however, and some of her miming is very poor. The sound is also far from perfect.

Recommended, if only for the music.

■ Maria Callas: *Life and Art*

Maria Callas, soprano; various interviewees.

Kultur, black & white and color, 1987, 78 minutes.

This documentary about the great Maria Callas, while not the last word, certainly belongs in every opera lover's collection. It begins inauspiciously, with the soprano's last accompanist, Robert Sutherland, strolling through her Paris apartment, musing over how the furniture was arranged. But within moments we see and hear Callas onstage at Covent Garden in 1964, singing a remarkable "Vissi d'arte" from *Tosca*, and then the interviews begin.

Franco Zeffirelli compares her to Nijinsky and Michelangelo, tenor Giuseppe di Stefano says she was the "queen of opera, but what she really wanted was to be the queen of jet society," and so on. By the close of this fascinating tape, we are a bit closer to understanding the artist and woman.

We learn about her early years, the start of her career, her peculiar marriage to Meneghini, her desire for fame and adulation. We note the triumphs and scandals, the distortions by the press, the entry of the woman, at the expense of the artist, into the jet set, the affair with tycoon Aristotle Onassis ("Why do you bother to sing?" he asked her. "I've got plenty of money").

Along the way we hear and see Callas onstage at the Paris Opéra singing "Una voce poco fa," more of the 1964 *Tosca*, a 1955 recording session of *Norma* under Tullio Serafin, a 1962 "Habanera," and bits of her 1974 tour with di Stefano.

Callas was riveting to watch and listen to in conversation as well as in song. We are left with a good look at her art, vulnerability, and sad decline. A new generation of singers and opera lovers will welcome the chance to view this tape.

■ Maria: *A Film about Maria Callas*

By Tony Palmer. John Ardoin, consultant; Tony Palmer, director

VAI, black & white and color, 1987, 90 minutes.

In this century, only a handful of opera singers have become household names, among them Caruso and Callas. In both cases, the timing was auspicious. Caruso came along at the turn of the century, just when the phonograph record was becoming popular. Callas arrived on the scene after World War II, when the cult of personality was finding a broader base as a by-product of television and the growing impact of the media.

Callas was the ideal subject for the postwar media, which was hungry for the exotic, the mysterious, and the dramatic. That she was a great singer who virtually revolutionized opera is almost beside the point; it was her temperamental, quixotic image that caught the public's imagination. In all, she sang 535 performances of 43 roles, plus a few dozen concerts. While only a certain number heard her in live performance, many more know the saga of her dramatic and sad life.

Tony Palmer has assembled visual and aural material from virtually every part of Callas's fifty-three years for this documentary. Beginning with shots of her infancy and childhood in New York and ending with photos taken of her in the street shortly before her death in Paris in 1977, Palmer interlaces everything with running commentary by people who knew her at each stage. A lifelong friend talks about Callas's girlish shyness. Franco Zeffirelli recalls her attachment to director Luchino Visconti. Critic John Ardoin says she didn't cancel performances as frequently as she has been reputed to do. A companion during her last days recounts her sad affair with Aristotle Onassis and how she looked on her deathbed. In between, Callas frequently speaks for herself, telling badgering reporters at airports that she doesn't want to give interviews, admitting toward the end that the voice is not what it used to be.

Palmer is weakest in his glossed-over treatment of her career at La Scala and of her working relationship with Tullio Serafin, the conductor who brought her to international fame. Callas insisted that the La Scala management engage him; later, when he recorded *Traviata* with another soprano, she dropped him as though she had never known him.

There are excerpts from some of her concerts, and a particularly compelling clip of her *Tosca* at Covent Garden. Vocally, one can see that her infamous wobble was apparently a deep-seated, inherent fault. It was not a matter of tension; her jaw remains relaxed in every shot. Dramatically, her gestures were not that unusual, but she knew how to combine them for an indescribable effect.

Although much of this material has been seen before in other documentaries, Palmer nicely captures Callas as a singer and a woman, showing how frequently they were at odds with each other. Callas fulfilled her enormous drive to become rich and famous, but she paid dearly for it.

■ Placido: *A Year in the Life of Placido Domingo*

Kultur, color, 1984, 105 minutes.

Although this documentary with music is as shallow as a teaspoon, it's a delight to watch. Placido Domingo is one of the world's greatest tenors and probably the hardest-working. He seems capable of being in two places at once, is rarely in anything but superlative voice, exudes charm, has begun an interesting if unspectacular conducting career, and apparently has a wife and children who adore him and vice versa. He is almost too good to be real.

True to its title, this tape takes us through a twelve-month period in Domingo's life. We see him at airports, signing autographs, and chatting with reporters. But there is also interesting rehearsal and performance footage of Domingo in excerpts from *Manon Lescaut, Tales of Hoffmann, La Fanciulla del West* (and conducting *Die Fledermaus*). We also see him in *Tosca, Otello,* and the Zeffirelli film of *La Traviata.*

Some entertaining nonoperatic moments include the taping of his TV specials with Carol Burnett and Charles Aznavour and his defense of his foray into popular music. Never less than affable, he is a great singer and a happy man—in a word, irresistible. If you aren't looking for any insights whatsoever, this is the cassette to have.

■ Nicolai Ghiaurov: *Tribute to a Great Basso*

Excerpts from operas by Gounod, Massenet, Mussorgsky, Puccini, Rossini, Verdi; Nicolai Ghiaurov, bass; Mirella Freni, soprano; José Carreras, tenor; Piero Cappuccilli, baritone; Claudio Abbado and Herbert von Karajan, conductors.

VIEW Video, color, 1986, 82 minutes.

This unnarrated documentary, made by Bulgarian TV, showcases the great Bulgarian bass Nicolai Ghiaurov in many of his finest roles. We also see him applying makeup, rehearsing, accepting applause, flying in planes, riding in cars, and admiring several cities. These nonmusical moments tend to bore, but the fast-forward control on the VCR can remedy this problem.

Along the way in this musical travelogue, extended excerpts from *Faust, Boris Godunov, Simon Boccanegra, The Barber of Seville, Don Quichotte,* and the Verdi Requiem serve to remind us what a natural, beautiful sound Ghiaurov possesses. The church scene from *Faust,* with Mirella Freni at her most winning as the terrified Marguerite, is particularly telling, although the arty camerawork and superimpositions add little. Other highlights include a touching death scene from *Don Quichotte* and a spectacular reading of Fiesco's aria from *Simon Boccanegra* (this excerpt alone defines great basso singing). Don Basilio's aria suffers from overproduction (there are sprites dancing around, presumably to represent the rumors in the text) but it is well sung. Brief glimpses of Carreras and Cappuccilli, and even briefer glimpses of Abbado and von Karajan, are merely bonuses. Ghiaurov is what counts, and he sounds marvelous.

In the review copy his voice was always just a bit out of sync with the prerecorded music, and the excerpts are cut off abruptly and unmusically. If the producers of this film had loved opera as much as they love Ghiaurov, this tape might have been superb. As it stands, the great basso's recordings are just as good or better.

■ *Tosca's Kiss*

A Film by Daniel Schmid.

VAI, color, 1985, 87 minutes. Italian with English subtitles.

This cassette is for somewhat specialized tastes, and one has to have more than a passing interest in both opera and human nature to fully appreciate it. Filmed in Milan at the Casa Verdi, a retirement home that the composer built for his operatic colleagues, this film is about music, old age, memories, and friendship, among other things. It's entertaining, moving, and enlightening.

The spirit of Giuseppe Verdi (whose royalties still help to keep the home afloat) is everywhere in evidence and though the many characters we meet revere him, they're also very much involved with their personal memories, their few glorious moments in the operatic sun. The film has many stars but focuses mainly on former soprano Sara Scuderi, now in her eighties. She is by turns girlish, sentimental, and wise, and her operatic reminiscences are charming and touching. All of Casa Verdi's inhabitants want to perform for director Schmid's camera and he lets them—with some wonderfully entertaining and hammy results—but it is Scuderi, infirm of step and clearly wearing a wig, who takes center stage.

Because the director doesn't play the film for sentimentality, the one manipulative moment is forgivable. It comes when Scuderi sings along with a fifty-year-old recording of herself performing "Vissi d'arte" from Puccini's *Tosca*. We're amazed at how much voice still comes out of the octogenarian diva, but even more impressive are her artistry and presence. Like the entire film, she is a life-affirming experience.

■ Shirley Verrett: *A Film Biography of the Black Diva*

Shirley Verrett, soprano; with Jon Vickers and Placido Domingo, tenors; Ruggero Raimondi, bass; various conductors and orchestras.

Kultur, color, 1985, 60 minutes.

This is a highly enjoyable, occasionally insightful hour spent with Shirley Verrett, but the subtitle is a misnomer. Verrett does discuss aspects of her early life in New Orleans and California, her religious upbringing, and her debt to Marian Anderson, but this is not a biography. It is a portrait of the diva—in rehearsal, performance, song, and interview—and has aspects at times of a travelogue and fashion show.

Verrett is very beautiful and articulate. Her thoughts about subjects like Callas, bad productions, and the Arena di Verona (which she likens to a football stadium) are interesting and amusing. She can also be a bit self-serving, but it's the music that counts here, and there's plenty of it.

Oddly, most of the vocal performances are nonoperatic. A couple of spirituals are nicely sung, and it's doubtful whether Richard Rodgers' "With a Song in My Heart" has ever sounded so lovely. "Hello Young Lovers," accompanied by shots of people strolling lovingly through the streets of Paris, is a bit overdone.

Verrett appears with Jon Vickers in *Samson and Delilah*, and we wish there were more of this Covent Garden production. There is a fabulous "Vissi d'arte" onstage in Verona and a scene from *Iphigénie en Tauride* at the Paris Opéra. La Scala offers some rehearsals for *Carmen*, the Habanera, and a discussion of why Verrett hates Piero Faggioni's production.

The voice-over narration is insipid and adulatory, but the film is nonetheless an interesting look at a fascinating woman and diva.

Opera: Humor and Satire

■ **P. D. Q. Bach (Peter Schickele):** *The Abduction of Figaro*

Michael Burt, Jack Walsh, Marilyn Brustadt, Lisbeth Lloyd, Will Roy, John Ferrante, LeRoy Lehr, Dana Krueger, Bruce Edwin Ford; Chorus, Corpse [*sic*] de Ballet, Orchestra of the Minnesota Opera, Prof. Peter Schickele, cond.

VAI, color, 1984, 144 minutes.

As most fans of classical music are aware, Peter Schickele "discovered" P. D. Q. Bach (admittedly the least important of J. S. Bach's children) and has been performing his "compositions" all over the world. *Abduction* is clearly his most ambitious. It is brilliantly—indeed, almost too brilliantly—contrived. A familiarity with rock and roll, folk songs, Gilbert and Sullivan, Mozart, ballet, and remnants of popular culture helps in getting the many musical jokes; the second-act ballet, for instance, is half *La Sylphide* and half Carmen Miranda. It's just a bit too much for any one person and assumes so much knowledge that there's a touch of snobbism to the entire undertaking. It's also an hour too long, and some of its crudities and appalling puns wear thin after a while. Schickele's penchant for slapstick also tends to get in the way of the musical satire. Still, there are enough funny moments to make a worthwhile evening's entertainment.

In fact, when it's good, it's very, very good. Donna Donna, one of the women chasing after Donald Giovanni, bears a remarkably close resemblance, as does her music, to the real Mozartean character, foibles and all. Her opening aria is a gem, and the takeoffs on the other Mozart characters are often on target and just as funny. The characters' names are irresistible: Shleporello, Pecadillo, Blondie, and Susanna Susannadanna, to name just a few.

119

Certainly, some people have never found Schickele particularly funny, but few have ever accused him of being ill-informed or superficial. Even real operas can be trying at two hours and twenty-four minutes, but when his jokes work they are hilarious and the tedious or repetitive moments can be skipped at will. There is fun to be had here, and the performances, needless to say, are beyond reproach.

■ *La Gran Scena Opera Company di New York*

Ira Siff, Philip Koch, Bruce Hopkins, Dennis Raley, Keith Jurosko, Luis Russinyol, others.

VAI, color, 1985, 112 minutes. All selections sung in their original languages.

Parodies of opera have to be knowledgeable to be funny, otherwise the parodists can appear mean-spirited or just plain stupid. It's all too easy to make fun of opera itself; in order for a parody to work it must come from within the music and the idiom—all the fun lies in the details. This one, taped at the Munich Theatre Festival in 1985, is ideal.

Here the prima donnas are not donnas. Most of the music has not been transposed (with an exception or two noted below). Instead, they use an augmented falsetto that reaches, with remarkable clarity, up to a high C-sharp. There's more than a touch of camp in this show, and so few viewers remain totally indifferent to it. Even if this type of show annoys you, the sheer artistry and sincerity of these chaps will hold your attention.

What better way to begin than with "The Ride of the Valkyries," and the sound could take the roof off Bayreuth. The recitative and aria from Handel's *Semele* follows (these "donnas" stray from the beaten path), with a battle ensuing between the star mezzo and the overly passionate comprimario soprano. Jokes aside, mezzo Philip Wanelle offers a real trill and accurate *fiorature*—there's real singing as well as real satire here.

The final duet from the first act of *La Bohème* is next, with Gabriella Tonnoziti-Casseruola ("the world's oldest living diva") and tenor Luis Russinyol. The group's leading diva, Mme. Vera Galupe-Borszkh (actually Ira Siff, the company's artistic director), then delivers a *Lucia* mad scene that will not soon be forgotten. Throughout, Siff throws in little vocal mannerisms from many of the great, recognizable Lucias of the recent past. There are plenty of in-jokes and subtleties for the aficionado to enjoy. Other highlights include the seguidilla from *Carmen*, the entire final act of *La Traviata*, and a tribute to Diana Ross that will make many opera singers think twice about "crossing over" into pop music.

There is much to chuckle over here, but unfortunately one member of the troupe acts as the hostess, "America's most beloved retired diva, Miss Sylvia Bills." The impersonation is in poor taste and, worse, isn't funny. If necessary, you can skip over these parts, but be careful not to miss the music.

■ *Anna Russell—The First Farewell Concert*

Anna Russell, *prima donna assoluta*; Robert Rosenberger, piano.

VAI, color, 1984, 85 minutes.

Anna Russell is one of a kind. Having made vain attempts to have an operatic career dozens of years ago (as the prima donna of the Ellis Island Opera Company, she claims), she soon settled in as the world's leading opera satirist. Her knowledge is vast, her voice used to be better (although she still sings soprano, contralto, tenor, and baritone on this tape), her delivery is of the garden-club-speaker-gone-berserk variety. She is a large, white-haired woman and in this performance, taped at the Baltimore Museum in November 1984, she wears an immense pink chiffon gown that makes her look like a large puff of cotton candy.

The program is made up of old favorites. After commenting on "wind instruments I have known," imitating many of them amusingly, she explains how she got the pink chiffon gown. But as her fans know, it is in her musical creativity and analysis that her real humor and talents lie, and a chance to savor them soon follows.

Her version of a Gilbert and Sullivan operetta is still brilliant. The plot is properly convoluted, and she sings all the parts—even the four-part madrigal—by herself. Her patter song is worth the whole evening. Her analysis of Wagner's Ring, which no other entertainer has ever dared to undertake, is infamous. She knows the plot and music inside out and reduces the sixteen-hour cycle to about twenty minutes, without leaving out any important elements.

The program ends with a series of folk tunes, including "Jolly Old Sigmund Freud," and she invites the audience to join her in some wonderfully gross noisemaking. News commentator Edwin Newman is in the audience, and he allows his dignity to fall flat for the occasion. An extremely good time is had by all.

Anna Russell in *Anna Russell: The First Farewell Concert* at the Baltimore Museum, November, 1984. Courtesy Video Artists International.

Opera: Special Programs and Films

■ Sherrill Milnes at Juilliard: *An Opera Master Class*

The Juilliard Master Class Series. Produced and directed by Peter Rosen.

Accompanist: Howard Lubin. A coproduction of Mistoke, Inc. and Peter Rosen Productions, Inc. In association with Herbert Barrett Management and the Juilliard School.

Home Vision, color, 1986, 75 minutes.

Toward the end of this master class, Sherrill Milnes speculates that very few of the vocal students at Juilliard (or anywhere else) will ever make their livings as singers. Most of them, he says, will sing only for the joy of it.

The thought is sobering, considering the abundant talents of the half-dozen students who sing for him, for the audience in Alice Tully Hall, and for the video cameras. Each of them has some potential, although none is a future Ponselle, Caruso, or Battistini.

While Milnes cannot pass on to students what is best about himself, he does manage to impart bits of shrewd vocal advice to a wide range of aspiring singers. At one point he even makes the audience stand up and go through a breathing exercise, just to demonstrate the mechanics of supporting the voice. Throughout, Milnes is a congenial, even inspiring, teacher.

The camerawork is decent and the editing purposeful—cutaway shots of the audience or of Milnes's reactions make this class an interesting video experience. In short, this is an entertaining show about vocal technique.

◼ *Silent Night with José Carreras*

José Carreras, tenor; Richard Osterreicher, musical arranger; Dietmar Dworschak, director.

Kultur, color, 1985, 40 minutes.

Brevity may be the soul of wit, but in the case of this Christmas bauble it is also the soul of charm. Beautifully filmed in and around a wintry Salzburg, this tape offers pleasant narration and a bevy of well-sung carols by José Carreras, who is at his most elegant and lyrical here.

Carreras rides in a sleigh, sings in the Salzburg cathedral and in front of the little chapel where "Silent Night" was first performed, and narrates a typically folksy Austrian Christmas celebration. The dreamlike atmosphere is heightened by misty shots of icicles and a countryside blanketed in snow.

Carreras sings "I'm Dreaming of a White Christmas" and, remarkably, avoids the operatic tone. He croons prettily, pronouncing the first word "Ah'm" in order to be totally casual about it (but mispronounces "sleigh" as "slee"). Schubert's "Ave Maria" and "Mille cherubini in coro" are superb, and he escapes the usual tenorial pitfalls by refusing to drag them out. "Adeste fideles," with chorus, is a model of dignity and piety, as is Mozart's "Ave verum corpus," and he actually makes "Jingle Bells" sound like a musical composition. "Silent Night," sung in German, Spanish, and English, is beautiful as well.

◼ *Puccini*

Starring Robert Stephens, Virginia McKenna, and Judith Howarth. Directed and edited by Tony Palmer; written by Charles Wood.

Home Vision, color, 1984, 113 minutes.

Giacomo Puccini's life could well have served him as a libretto. Tony Palmer and Charles Wood have singled out what is perhaps its most dramatic incident and turned it into a striking film.

The story concerns a scandal caused by the jealous rage of Elvira, Puccini's wife, over his presumed affair with Doria Manfredi, a young servant in the Puccini household. Although Puccini had a highly active libido, he was evidently innocent of this particular dalliance. But Elvira would not be placated, and the harrassed girl ultimately committed suicide.

It is a sad story, well directed by Palmer and vividly acted by Robert Stephens as the composer, Virginia McKenna as his wife, and Judith Howarth as the serving girl. Stephens is especially effective as the wildly successful Puccini whose private life is less than happy. We enjoy his half-wistful, half-weary monologues as much as the many arias and melodies that make up the background music.

Less effective is the intercutting into the story of scenes of preparation for a modern-day production of *Turandot* by the Scottish Opera. Tony Palmer, the director of *Puccini*, happens also to be the director of the new opera production. Accordingly, the camera follows him around during the documentary scenes. These rehearsal scenes slowly reveal what looks like a ghastly production taking shape; later, when Palmer reads excerpts from the reviews, the critics bear out our suspicions.

The rationale for this intercutting is never made clear—it serves only to halt the action and vitiate the dramatic tension in the Puccini story. This is an interesting, odd film, but less than completely satisfying.

■ *The Life of Verdi*

Ronald Pickup, Carla Fracci. Renato Castellani, director.

Kultur, color, 1986, four cassettes, 600 minutes.

This epic biography was produced by the BBC, Italian radio, and German TV, and the result is highly successful, if too long. Filmed in Italy, Leningrad, Paris, and London, the ten-hour miniseries cost approximately a million dollars an hour and used over 100 actors and 18,000 extras. With that as background, it could easily have been a spectacular bore, but, in fact, the film is intelligent, thoughtful, and entertaining.

Born in 1813, Giuseppe Verdi died in 1901, and in some ways defines nineteenth-century music. It is for this reason that the excerpts from his music should have been longer. We are presented instead with a well-done biography with a few musical examples, some of them sung by the likes of Callas, Tebaldi, and Pavarotti.

The cast is excellent, especially the two leads. Ronald Pickup, of Britain's National Theatre, is superb. He has the skill to play a difficult and complicated man over a sixty-year period and make the character valid and all of a piece. Giuseppina Strepponi, the composer's wife, is played by ballerina Carla Fracci. Those familiar with her dancing will not be surprised by her grace and expressiveness, but her grasp of the nuances of this complex character's personality displays far more dramatic ability than expected.

This is a thoughtful biography that never descends into sentimentality or belabors a point. Director Renato Castellani manages the international cast so well that we hardly realize that some actors are speaking English while others have been dubbed. The production is well mounted and quite sumptuous.

Verdi lovers will enjoy this film.

TWO

DANCE ON VIDEOCASSETTE

Dance: Ballet and Modern

■ American Ballet Theatre at the Met

Les Sylphides: Music by Chopin, choreography by Michel Fokine. Marianna Tcherkassky, Cynthia Harvey, Cheryl Yeager, Mikhail Baryshnikov, soloists. Sylvia—Pas de Deux: Music by Delibes, choreography by George Balanchine. Martine van Hamel, Patrick Bissell, soloists. Triad: Music by Prokofiev, choreography by Kenneth MacMillan. Robert La Fosse, Johan Renvall, Amanda McKerrow, soloists. Paquita—Grand Pas: Music by Minkus, choreography by Natalia Makarova after Marius Petipa. Cynthia Gregory, Fernando Bujones, Susan Jaffe, Cynthia Harvey, Leslie Browne, Dierdre Carberry, soloists. Corps de ballet of the American Ballet Theatre.

HBO Video, color, 1984, 100 minutes.

This program, taped live at the Metropolitan Opera House in New York on June 11, 1984, was clearly designed to show off the company to best advantage, and it does. It is a delightful 100 minutes, with intermissions at the viewer's discretion.

TV director Brian Large has not disappointed us. In a mixed program like this one, the director must know the works well—Triad and Les Sylphides have nothing in common except their vocabulary of movement—and, indeed, we see all there is to see. Les Sylphides is a lovely, delicate work, the quintessential "effortless" classical ballet. Baryshnikov, the lone male dancer, is understated throughout, and his musicality is obvious in all he does. His pas de deux with the stylish Marianna Tcherkassky is dreamy and reserved. Cynthia Harvey performs her solo seemingly without touching the stage, and Cheryl Yeager's mazurka is technically proficient without actually being inspired. The corps is lovely, and Paul Connelly conducts sympathetically.

The pas de deux from *Sylvia* is superbly danced by the long-limbed Martine van Hamel, who brings elegance to whatever she dances. Watching sturdy, handsome Patrick Bissell in action makes his untimely death seem all the more cruel. His athletic leaps and turns and empathetic partnering will be missed. Alan Barker helps to bring Delibes' score to life, and Balanchine's choreography is as effective now as it was when it was created in 1972.

Triad is a poetic 1972 work by Kenneth MacMillan, about a boy's complicated feelings when his brother becomes involved with a girl. Robert La Fosse uses his prodigious technique to serve the drama, and Johan Renvall as the older brother is only slightly less impressive. The role of the girl should be taken by a great dancer, and while Amanda McKerrow is attractive and dances competently she lacks the specialness the part needs to come alive. Her three male companions are well danced by John Gardner, John Turjoman, and Craig Wright. Conductor Alan Barker brings out the best in Prokofiev's score, and special mention should be made of Dennis Cleveland's handsome violin solo.

Paquita, cream puff that it is, is well served, too. Leslie Browne needs a bit more elevation, but her balance, line, and landings cannot be faulted. Dierdre Carberry dazzles with her flashing, grand jetés. Cynthia Harvey is lovely in her harp-accompanied variation. Only Susan Jaffe is a bit off form. All attention, of course, is focused on Cynthia Gregory and Fernando Bujones, and they're at their best. Bujones is his most classically correct self (if in the guise of a peacock), but he deserves the ovations he receives. Gregory is a miracle. Imposingly tall, she dances with superb technical certainty, and her thirty-two fouettés in the finale are flawless. Once again, Paul Connelly conducts with flair.

If you want to see ABT at its best, buy or rent this tape.

■ *American Ballet Theatre in San Francisco*

Airs: Music by Handel, choreography by Paul Taylor. Lisa Rinehart, Christine Spizzo, Kristine Soleri, Anna Spelman, Peter Fonesca, Johan Renvall, Thomas Titone, soloists. *Jardin aux Lilas:* Music by Chausson, choreography by Anthony Tudor. Leslie Browne, Robert La Fosse, Martine van Hamel, Michael Owen, soloists. *The Black Swan Pas de Deux:* Music by Tchaikovsky, choreography by Marius Petipa. Cynthia Gregory, Fernando Bujones, soloists. *Romeo and Juliet—Balcony Scene:* Music by Prokofiev, choreography by Kenneth MacMillan. Natalia Makarova, Kevin McKenzie, soloists. *Great Galloping Gottschalk:* Music by Gottschalk, choreography by Lynne Taylor-Corbett. Various soloists and corps. Paul Connelly and Alan Barker, conds.

Home Vision, color, 1985, 105 minutes.

This performance, taped on March 1, 1985, less than a year after HBO Video's *American Ballet Theatre at the Met*, is a nice companion piece to the earlier tape. Together, they offer a valid view of the company as it was performing at the time. The quality is remarkably high, and the styles are interestingly diverse. The New York performances are more impressive, although some of the credit for that must go to TV director Brian Large's somewhat better way with the Met than with the War Memorial Opera House (although neither space is ideally suited to ballet). Be that as it may, this present tape is nothing to dismiss.

Paul Taylor's *Airs* is an entertaining 1978 piece set to some of Handel's loveliest music. As usual with this choreographer's work, this is a joyous celebration of dance for dance's sake—the leaping and posing in the second movement are fascinating. The discerning viewer will notice some of Martha Graham's influence but, of course, this lacks her austerity. All the dancers do good work in this marvelous piece, but Peter Fonesca and Johan Renvall are especially outstanding.

Having what some believe to be Anthony Tudor's greatest ballet on tape is another real gift. *Jardin* has always been a complicated piece: a girl forced into a marriage of convenience must say farewell to her lover, while her fiancé's mistress seeks another few minutes with *him*. The smoldering passions beneath the conventionality are all too clear—this is a heartrending work. Leslie Browne does not quite have the tragic stature to handle the role of the girl, but Martine van Hamel, as the other woman, is both majestic and menacing. Robert La Fosse is moving as the girl's rejected lover, and the fiancé is danced with proper distance by Michael Owen. The supporting cast is excellent.

The so-called *Black Swan* pas de deux never quite seems to work out of context, and despite some virtuoso turns by Gregory and Bujones, this extract is no exception. Both performers are great dancers and at their most gloriously secure here. Gregory's coolness, however, is a bit overdone, while Bujones seems arrogant beyond stardom, almost as though he were in another galaxy. Somehow, the resulting performance strikes no sparks. Not so the balcony scene from *Romeo and Juliet* as danced by

Makarova and McKenzie. Her line is pure, and her acting is totally convincing. The whole performance has a matchless spontaneity and energy; Thomas Skelton's evocative lighting helps, too, and Brian Large knows this work well enough to make it highly effective on the small screen.

The rambunctious *Great Galloping Gottschalk*, which closes the program, is a real crowd-pleaser. Lynne Taylor-Corbett's choreography is fun, although without much inventiveness. The opening movement has a nice, sultry quality, with Elaine Kudo in fine form, while Susan Jaffe and Robert La Fosse are excellent in the second movement. The next movement, with Gil Boggs and Johan Renvall, is nicely clownish and athletic but has little substance. The finale is much too rushed and busy, and Gottschalk's rather mediocre music (well arranged by Jack Elliott) doesn't help offset the work's flimsiness.

This tape has much to offer, but if you can own only one ABT combination program, it should be HBO Video's.

■ *Anna Karenina*

Maya Plisetskaya, Alexander Godunov, Vladimir Tikhonov, Yuri Vladimirov; Orchestra of the Bolshoi Theatre, Moscow, Yuri Simonov, cond. Music by Rodion Shchedrin, choreography by Maya Plisetskaya.

Kultur, color, 1974, 81 minutes.

Based on Tolstoy's novel, *Anna Karenina* (1972) was the first ballet choreographed by Maya Plisetskaya. Lovers of ballet or of Russian literature may be disappointed, however.

As we all know, *Anna Karenina* tells a good story. Plisetskaya, however, has decided to concentrate on what is going on in Anna's head. There is a great deal of internalizing and soul-searching, and unless one recalls the novel scene by scene, it's a challenge to figure out the plot. Furthermore, Shchedrin (Plisetskaya's husband) has composed a lushly romantic score that lacks any real character.

But Plisetskaya could probably dance the world's most banal story and still delight and amaze us. Knowing her own strengths, she has choreographed a work that shows off all her technical and emotive qualities. The Vronsky of Alexander Godunov is technically assured and attractive, and he treats the work with respect. Vladimir Tikhonov is a cruel Karenin, and Yuri Vladimirov makes more of the Stationmaster's role than is ever in

Maya Plisetskaya in the Bolshoi Ballet production of *Anna Karenina*. Courtesy Kultur Video.

the novel: here Plisetskaya (Anna) sees him as an evil coconspirator in the plot against her. The Bolshoi orchestra is in the able hands of conductor Yuri Simonov.

Since this is a filmed version, the camera is used to great advantage. The production is not stagebound and the action moves outdoors with fluidity.

In short, a minor work, danced by major stars.

■ *Anyuta*

Ekaterina Maximova, Vladimir Vasiliev, Gali Abaidulov. Music by Valery Gavrilin. Choreography by Vladimir Vasiliev.

Kultur, color, 1982, 68 minutes.

■ *Macbeth*

Alexei Fadeyechev, Nina Timofeyeva, Valeri Anisimov. Music by Kirill Molchanov. Choreography by Vladimir Vasiliev.

Kultur, color, 1984, 105 minutes.

These two releases are for dance specialists only. Both ballets are unknown outside of the Soviet Union, and neither one is a masterpiece. They do prove, however, that Vasiliev, one of the greatest Soviet dancers, is a more than capable choreographer. In *Anyuta*, which is based on a double-edged story by Chekhov about an independent woman who marries a petty bureaucrat, Vasiliev also dances the role of the drunk but loving father. This gentle and moving work has some funny moments, and Maximova dances brilliantly as the sassy wife. Abaidulov, as the bureaucrat, is suitably stuffy, and Valery Gavrilin's music, although hardly memorable, is melodic and atmospheric.

The *Macbeth* misses the mark. It is too long, for one thing. Plus Vasiliev has seriously misread the character of Lady Macbeth, seeing her as half-crazed from the start. As a result, the plot loses its dramatic force. Timofeyeva, however, dances rivetingly, and so, even if it isn't Shakespeare, her portrayal is fascinating. As Macbeth, Fadeyechev is superb—ferocious at the start, crawling to his throne in fear at the end. It's hard to take the new ending, in which the witches drive Macbeth to suicide, and the music is forgettable.

These are essentially Vasiliev's shows. They may not be ballets for the ages, but they're worth seeing at least once. The Soviets still keep a great deal of their work to themselves, and this tape offers a more rounded view of their efforts.

■ *Baryshnikov by Tharp*

Mikhail Baryshnikov, Elaine Kudo, members of the American Ballet Theatre; Don Mischer, producer; Don Mischer and Twyla Tharp, directors.

Kultur, color, 1984, 59 minutes.

It would be a challenge to find someone who does not like either Baryshnikov or Tharp, and this cassette (originally produced for Public

Television) brings them together in three wonderfully entertaining ballets.

The show is framed as a "stroll" by Baryshnikov through the "dance alphabet," with stops at each letter as he charmingly explains or demonstrates a ballet term. The first dance work, *The Little Ballet*, is to music by Alexander Glazounov and is a lyrical, traditional piece, in which the star and four dancers go through elegant, romantic movements, some with an occasional ironic smile. It's a perfect curtain raiser.

The second ballet, *Sinatra Suite*, is set to five songs by Frank Sinatra and is superbly performed by Baryshnikov and Elaine Kudo. Dressed in black against a dark blue backdrop lighted by Art Deco lamps, the work is in the best Fred Astaire–Cyd Charisse tradition, infused with Tharp's special brand of zaniness and a touch of apache dancing.

The final work is the well-known *Push Comes to Shove*, with music by Joseph Lamb and Franz Josef Haydn. Funny and creative, it uses a bowler hat as a prop and is all about ballet, posing, and classical (and not so classical) attitudes. It's a gem.

We're left at the close of this show with the feeling that Baryshnikov's dancing knows no limits. This tape will appeal to everyone, not just balletomanes.

■ *Black Tights*

Cyd Charisse, Moira Shearer, Zizi Jeanmaire, Roland Petit, others. Choreographed by Roland Petit, introduced by Maurice Chevalier. Directed by Terence Young.

VAI, color, 1962, 126 minutes.

Roland Petit was a popularist in the way that Twyla Tharp is; he has the same sense of humor and tends to mix and match different styles of dance. This tape of four Petit ballets presents a good picture of his talents, both as a choreographer and as a dancer.

Zizi Jeanmaire performs with Petit in his justly famous version of *Carmen*, and both are stylish and provocative. *La Croqueuse de Diamants* ("The Diamond Cruncher"), too, is a delight: Jeanmaire sings and dances with relish in this tongue-in-cheek ballet about jewel thieves who attempt to stop her from eating some stolen diamonds. Also top-notch is *Deuil en 24 Heures*. Here we can understand just what made this long-legged, elegant, and pliable performer such a special dancer. Less successful is Petit's

Cyrano de Bergerac, in which he partners Moira Shearer, but without great distinction; the ballerina was past her prime when this was filmed.

The costumes by Yves Saint Laurent and the sets by Georges Wakhevitch are splendid. It is interesting to note that Gérard Lemaitre and Hans Van Manen, who later became artistic directors of the Netherlands Dance Theatre, appear to very good advantage in this film. This is a collector's item, a fine visual document of an interesting choreographer's and dancer's work.

■ The Catherine Wheel

Music by David Byrne, choreography by Twyla Tharp. Sarah Rudner, Jennifer Way, Tom Rawe, Katie Glasner, Raymond Kurshals, Shelley Washington, Christine Uchida, soloists. With an introduction by Twyla Tharp. Music performed by David Byrne. Production designed by Santo Loquasto; computer animation by Rebecca Allen.

HBO Video, color, 1982, 87 minutes.

This is a specially-made-for-television version of a work premiered on Broadway in 1981 to great acclaim (Arlene Croce hailed it as "a major event in our theatre"). Time has apparently dimmed its luster.

It isn't that the transfer to TV is not effective; in fact, it's just the opposite. The animation is entertaining, as are the reverse-action and odd camera angles. It is more a case of the work's proving somewhat pretentious, an uncomfortable cross between the very serious and the very playful.

This ballet is "about" St. Catherine, a fourth-century martyr who strove for perfection and died on a spiked wheel. Heavily symbolic, it uses the pineapple as a motif, which in silhouette looks like a grenade or a mushroom cloud. The dancers, aside from the solo dancer who attempts to emulate the perfection of the computerized, animated Catherine figure, are a family at war with one another. They wear odd clothes and have a maid who makes faces and a pet. Much of the dancing is too self-conscious, rather like the same choreographer's work in the movie *Amadeus* and totally unlike her brilliant *Push Comes to Shove*. The family business is too zany, the emotions too unsubtle.

In the work's two final movements, Tharp seems to settle down to the business at hand—dancing, rather than allegory for the ages—it's superb stuff. "Equilibrium Restored," the next-to-last movement, has a just-off-the-beat order to it that is exactly right for the moment, and the dancers use their arms with great expression. The final movement, "The Golden Section," contains the work's most beautiful choreography. One can only hope that some inventive ballet companies will excerpt the work.

The troupe always performs well. Special praise goes to Sarah Rudner as the Leader (who emulates Catherine), Shelley Washington as the spunky Maid, and Christine Uchida, who plays the Pet. The rest of the dancers, too, are excellent. David Byrne's music is, at times, rock minimalism; he has an enormous musical vocabulary and he shows it off well. Santo Loquasto's dazzling designs are as hip as the dance without being self-serving. Rebecca Allen's animation is good.

You might want to take a look at this one, just to see how one of America's finest choreographers can go wrong and, ultimately, redeem herself.

■ Le Chat Botté (Puss in Boots)

Music by Tchaikovsky (arranged and orchestrated by John Lanchbery); choreography by Roland Petit. Patrick Dupond, Dominique Khalfouni, Jean-Pierre Aviotte, Jean-Charles Verchère. National Ballet of Marseilles.

Home Vision, color, 1986, 90 minutes.

It would be nice if this ballet could replace *Nutcracker* as a children's favorite. It is funnier, more charming, easier to follow, and contains more virtuoso dancing. A delightful adaptation of Charles Perrault's fairy tale, it concerns Jean, a farmer's son who inherits only a cat, with whom he becomes great friends. In the course of the ballet the cat meets a Princess, her little brother, and her ladies-in-waiting, and manages to have the Princess and Jean meet. No sooner do they fall in love than the Princess is kidnapped by a terrible ogre. (The contraption that both represents and houses the ogre and his retinue has to be seen to be believed; Josef Svoboda's designs are marvelously inventive.) Of course, the cat outwits the ogre, and Jean and his Princess get back together in what can only be called a knockdown pas de deux.

In between, there's plenty of dancing. The corps takes on many guises—as peasants, as the ogre's grotesque retinue, and as the royal courtiers—all, of course, in very different styles. The ogre, in red fright wig and hideous makeup, does some quite unballetic steps: he stands on his head, crawls like a snake, and moonwalks à la Michael Jackson. It's sinister and very effective.

One of the Paris Opéra Ballet's greatest *étoiles*, Patrick Dupond, dances the Cat. Kittenish, wise, and playful, he does as much with his hands and bewhiskered face as he does with his body. Jean-Pierre Aviotte and Dominique Khalfouni are a sweet pair of lovers, and Jean-Charles Verchère is the ogre in a brilliantly wicked portrayal. The corps is excellent throughout.

The picture is very good, as are the camera angles, but the sound leaves a great deal to be desired (though the review copy may have been flawed). This cassette is a joy and belongs in any ballet collection that leaves room for fun.

■ Coppélia

Fernando Bujones, with the Ballets de San Juan. Directed by Zeida Cecilia Mendez.

Kultur, color, 1987, 81 minutes.

Bujones is a dance phenomenon. He appears here as guest artist with the Puerto Rican company the Ballets de San Juan. The Swanilda is danced by Ana Maria Castanon, principal soloist with the company. (The preview tape has a Spanish introduction and plot synopsis between the acts. Presumably, the film will be dubbed in English before its release).

The performance was filmed before a live audience—and a lively one at that—that laughs, applauds, gasps and shouts with joy at the comic bits and at every leap from Bujones. The production is thoroughly professional, with some nicely disciplined dancing by the corps and excellent individual variations. The sets evoke a dollhouse, quite appropriate to Coppélia, but perhaps because the ballet was filmed in the theatre during performance, the lighting is inadequate.

Naturally, the only reason for making this video (or for owning it) is Bujones, who performs with immense charm and excitement. He seems altogether thrilled to be sharing his amazing leaps with us, almost pausing in midair. His spectacular first act is easily equalled by the incredible jetés and tours à la seconde in the third act. We can only lament that this ballet is much more the property of the female than of the male dancers.

Ana Maria Castanon is not up to the international standard of her partner, but her gallant performance is perfectly in tune with the role of Swanilda—ingratiating, perky, and just temperamental enough. The third-act divertissements are well danced, and the ballet ends in a blaze of Bujones.

This is a perfect matinee *Coppélia*, staged, costumed, and mounted intelligently. Were it not for the limitations of small screen viewing, it would be suitable for a school audience.

■ *Don Quixote (Kitri's Wedding)*

Mikhail Baryshnikov, Cynthia Harvey, Susan Jaffe, Patrick Bissell, with the American Ballet Theatre. Music by Ludwig Minkus, choreography by Mikhail Baryshnikov, after Gorsky and Petipa. Directed for television by Brian Large.

HBO Video, color, 1982, 86 minutes.

Much of the folkloric component of Don Quixote is reduced or eliminated in this version of the ballet. In other words, here we have a "modernized" Don Quixote—pure dance, not spectacle or even story, counts. Although the Don is a main character in this version, his importance is less crucial, and his personality is less developed.

The main reason to see this video is Baryshnikov's work, both as dancer and choreographer. What emerges is a balanced, clean, swiftly moving, and uncomplicated story, with plenty of well-designed solo and ensemble work. Baryshnikov's vision of *Don Quixote* may be emotionally less involving, yet the sweetness of the love between Kitri and Basil shines through and dancers such as Patrick Bissell (Espada), Susan Jaffe (Mercedes), Robert La Fosse, and Gregory Osborn show off their skills to great advantage.

As Basil, Baryshnikov is a relaxed, rather earthy barber. Perhaps he is so amazing just because his preparation is so nonchalant. There are those who can compete with him for purely acrobatic values, yet the unique charm of his work lies more in his energy and perfect poise.

Cynthia Harvey's Kitri is more innocent than vixenish, although she does have spirit. She is also stylish, correct, and crisp, though a few dips in stamina cause her to cut short an attitude once or twice. Susan Jaffe displays her bravura technique with ingratiating demeanor; though her work does not stir any depths, she is superb in what is called for here. Bissell disappoints a bit. He seems unfocused and bland here.

The straightforward production was recorded live at the Metropolitan Opera House. The camera generally remains at stage level, affording a close, undistorted picture of the dancers, and the scenery is suitably handsome.

This interesting version of an old story deserves serious consideration by the balletomane, as much for Baryshnikov's dancing as for what he has cut, simplified, and modernized in this classic ballet.

■ Don Quixote

Rudolf Nureyev, Robert Helpmann, Lucette Aldous, with dancers of the Australian Ballet. Music by Ludwig Minkus, choreography by Nureyev after Gorsky and Petipa. Directed by Rudolf Nureyev and Robert Helpmann.

Kultur, color, 1973, 110 minutes.

This is ballet as spectacle, a filmed production lavishly staged and much heralded when first released. It is a version of the Gorsky-Petipa *Don Quixote* restaged by Nureyev for the 1970 Adelaide Festival of Arts. A full-blown, Kirov-style performance, it includes a great number of folk and gypsy *danses générales* and variations, comic pantomimes and a virtuosic pas de deux by the two principals.

Beginning with enormous energy, the pace of the production never flags, yet still manages a fine balance between the folkloric and the classical idiom. Lucette Aldous (as Kitri and the Duchess) embodies the character of a flirtatious, perky, but intelligent and tough-minded Kitri. She is very much up to the role, handling its bravura dancing with confidence and brio, though not quite a match for Nureyev.

Nureyev easily takes on the boyish, zesty, mischievous lineaments of the barber, Basil, overacting just a touch, but charmingly so. His dancing is supremely confident, radiant with poise and power and, in the opening scenes, almost frenetic in its energy. In his great solo variations his speed, lift, and line are marvelous; and his partnering is never less than sympathetic and rock-solid. His dazzling speed, his barrel turns, and the beauty of his extension are uncanny. His is an elegant and aristocratic conception of the role.

Robert Helpmann's Don Quixote is a wasted, almost demonic figure, obsessed and with a self-conscious look of fiery virtue. Ever the arrogant aristocrat, he exacts deference, service, and gratitude in spite of his delusions. No sickly sentimental Don this, but a commanding figure who almost requires humiliation yet still embodies knightly dignity and conviction.

The rest of the cast perform creditably enough. Sets and costumes are elaborate yet convincing. Cinematographer Geoffrey Unsworth occasionally goes for overhead shots, fade-ins, and superimpositions that distract from the dancing itself.

Unfortunately, the color values of the film have not stood up well over the years. In the early acts, the light-colored stage floor makes it next to impossible to follow the dancers' steps, and the tones seem to have gone over a bit far into the yellow end of the spectrum.

All in all, this is a noteworthy and thrilling version of a classic of the Russian-Spanish genre. With caveats as noted, it is definitely worth genuine consideration for the serious collector.

■ *An Evening with Ballet Rambert*

Ballet Rambert; choreography by Christopher Bruce and Robert North. Produced and directed by Thomas Grimm.

Home Vision, color, 1985, 98 minutes.

This tape consists of three modern ballets performed by Britain's oldest dance company, Ballet Rambert, founded in 1926. A glance at this tape will show that it has much to offer in terms of style that, while firmly based in classical ballet, has, at least in the three dances presented here, found its own very modern look.

Lonely Town, Lonely Street, choreographed by Robert North and set to the blues songs of Bill Withers, is a jazzy depiction of street scenes and life, and the company seems right at home with it. The movement is sexy and the dancers' faces and shoulders work as hard as the rest of their bodies. *Intimate Pages*, a moody, highly charged piece set to Janáček's Second String Quartet, is angular and abstract and has overtones of Martha Graham's style. The most entertaining ballet is *Sergeant Early's Dreams*, set to a suite of twelve American and British folk songs, played on whistles, fiddles, concertina, guitar, and other instruments, and sung by four singers. It portrays three very tipsy men and the trouble—some of it very funny—that they get into.

There is no need to single out any dancer for particular praise; the entire company is well integrated and wonderfully energetic. Home Vision's sound is substandard, but otherwise, this tape is recommended.

■ *An Evening with the Bolshoi*

Les Sylphides: Music by Chopin, choreography by Michel Fokine. Natalia Bessmertnova, Lyudmila Semenyaka, Nina Semizorova, Aleksei Fadeyechev, soloists. *Spartacus, Act II:* Music by Khachaturian, choreography by Yuri Grigorovich. Erek Moukhamedov, Natalia Bessmertnova, Aleksei Lazarev, Alla Mikhalchenko, soloists. *The Sleeping Beauty, Pas de Deux:* Music by Tchaikovsky, choreography by Marius Petipa. Nina Ananiashvili, Leonid Nikonov, soloists. *La Bayadère, Variations:* Music by Minkus, choreography by Marius Petipa. Mikhail Tsivin, soloist. *Swan Lake, Black Swan Pas de Deux:* Music by Tchaikovsky, choreography by Marius Petipa and Yuri Grigorovich. Nina Semizorova, Aleksei Fadeyechev, soloists. *Spring Waters:* Music by Rachmaninov, choreography by Asaf Messerer. Maria Bylova, Leonid Nikonov, soloists. *The Golden Age, Adagio:* Music by Shostakovich, choreography by Yuri Grigorovich. Erek Moukhamedov, Natalia Bessmertnova, soloists. *Don Quixote, Grand Pas:* Music by Minkus, choreography by Alexander Gorsky. Lyudmila Semenyaka, Yuri Vasyuchenko, soloists. The Bolshoi Ballet, the Orchestra of London, Alexander Kopylov, cond.

Home Vision, color, 1986, 120 minutes.

Although this is an exciting, if exhausting, evening of ballet, the real reason for wanting this tape is the dancing of Erek Moukhamedov and Natalia Bessmertnova. They are probably the Soviet Union's greatest soloists, and their dancing fairly takes one's breath away.

They are together in the second act of *Spartacus*, the wonderfully glitzy Grigorovich ballet created for Vasiliev, and in an excerpt from the same choreographer's *The Golden Age*. In the former, Bessmertnova is lovely as the sad, loyal Phrygia, but it is Moukhamedov's show. Both his technique and involvement seem to have become stronger since the 1984 taping of the entire ballet (available on HBO Video), although he was superb then as well. But here he is terrifying in his commitment, and his leaps are high and perfectly executed. His one-arm lifts of Bessmertnova seem like a magic act. In *The Golden Age* adagio, the starring couple are dreamy in their white costumes against a blue background, and they show us an entirely different and equally noteworthy facet of their capabilities.

The rest of the program is good without ever quite reaching greatness.

Les Sylphides is well served but does not enchant. Bessmertnova is again in her glory, but Semenyaka is off form, Semizorova seems uninvolved, and Aleksei Fadeyechev has the energy but looks like a wrestler. The excerpt from *The Sleeping Beauty* finds Nina Ananiashvili dancing handsomely, with great aplomb. Leonid Nikonov partners her well, but neither dancer presents a sense of character.

Mikhail Tsivin dances the brief *Bayadère* variations like a boy, lacking grand gestures and sweep, but his leaps are more than impressive. In the *Black Swan* pas de deux, Nina Semizorova is an arrogant Odile—without the thirty-two fouettés (this is Grigorovich's choreography), and Fadeyechev still looks odd but his rock-solid landings are impressive. *Spring Waters* seems like a work for enthusiastic, very young, and sprightly dancers. Maria Bylova and Nikonov are exhilarating.

The Grand Pas from *Don Quixote* is danced very quickly, and Yuri Vasyuchenko outdances Semenyaka: what he lacks in elevation he more than makes up for in speed and elegance.

Alexander Kopylov and the Orchestra of London are to be commended. The director, Stanislav Lushin, has made an odd camera choice—the long shots show too much of the top rim of the orchestra pit. If the whole evening had been better one might not have noticed, but the only time the dancing ever really catches fire is when Moukhamedev and Bessmertnova are onstage. This is for *their* fans, although the *Spartacus* excerpt makes it worthwhile for everyone.

■ *La Fille Mal Gardée*

Lesley Collier, Michael Coleman, Brian Shaw, Garry Grant, with the Royal Ballet. Choreography by Frederick Ashton after the scenario of Jean Dauberval. Music by Ferdinand Hérold, arranged and adapted by John Lanchbery. Orchestra of the Royal Opera House, conducted by John Lanchbery.

HBO Video, color, 1981, 98 minutes.

La Fille Mal Gardée may be the oldest ballet still in the repertory, having been premiered in Paris in 1803. This is a video of a live performance from Covent Garden—possibly a matinee, given the number of children caught as the camera pans the audience. In fact, this could be a nice, simple introductory ballet experience for youngsters, with its agreeable fairytale quality.

In Frederick Ashton's working of the story, there are some amusing touches, including one white miniature pony; four "chickens" and a pompous "rooster" who dance with henlike absurdity; an airborne exit for Garry Grant as Alain, the witless suitor; and Brian Shaw doing the mother's part with comic relish.

There is a sweet, fresh-air atmosphere to the ballet. The scenery is pleasantly two-dimensional, and the ballet features dances derived from the rhythms of rural life. The story is one of innocent love threatened by the ambitions of avaricious parents who try to marry Lise off to Alain, a rich buffoon who will eventually be scorned.

The two lovers, charmingly danced by Lesley Collier and Michael Coleman, do a good job of presenting the picture of romantic, lively, flirtatious young love. They have some very pleasing pas de deux in the first and third acts, along with solo variations. Collier has a chance to show off a great many intricate combinations, particularly in the short tambourine dance she does in the third act, while the amiable Coleman has a couple of nicely turned solos. Garry Grant, adorned with a Harpo Marx wig, provides some of the wittiest and most ingenious dancing.

Everything is quite obviously sunny, except for the marvelously fake thunderstorm with its orchestral effects of lightning, thunder, and rain. There is just enough suggestion of conflict to keep the saccharine from overpowering us, although *La Fille Mal Gardée* will never be more than a charming divertissement—nor should it be.

So, for the young at heart, lovers of fairy tales, and admirers of Frederick Ashton's whimsy and clean style, this is a fine production.

■ *Gaîté Parisienne*

Music by Jacques Offenbach (arranged by Manuel Rosenthal); choreography by Leonide Massine. Alexandra Danilova, Frederic Franklin, Leon Danielian, soloists; the Ballets Russes de Monte Carlo. A film by Victor Jessen.

VAI, black & white, 1954, 38 minutes.

This is a delicious memento of the Ballets Russes and particularly of Danilova, whose only filmed performance this is. The story of how it came about is outlandish and fun as well: Victor Jessen, a balletomane mad about *Gaîté* and Danilova, wanted to preserve her on film in this role, which was one of her greatest successes. Therefore, between 1944 and

1954 he attended dozens of performances of the work and filmed it in thirty-second takes. He sat in different seats in different theatres, secretly taking and retaking snippets, until, in 1954, he finally had it all on film and edited. He then tape recorded the score, later incorporating it into the film. Good for Jessen—his work paid off handsomely.

Gaîté Parisienne is not a masterpiece but, rather, a short work chock-full of rambunctiousness and sentimentality in equal doses, and when the three principals are dancing—which is almost always—it's a grand good time. It's about a life-loving glove seller (Danilova) and a lusty Peruvian (Danielian) who appear to fall in love in a café in Paris. They dance the night away, but the glove seller gives her heart to a romantic and wealthy Baron (Franklin). The performance here is wonderful—full of life and love—and the three leads are in great form, which is remarkable, considering that the film encompasses ten years. Although the rest of the cast changes (it's fun to chart the variations), the generally high level attests to the quality of the company.

The film is anything but perfect, and neither is the sound, but who cares? There's nothing quite like this. Recommended.

■ *Giselle*

Galina Mezentseva, Konstantin Zaklinsky, other soloists; with dancers of the Kirov Ballet. Music by Adolph Adam. Choreography by Jean Coralli and Jules Perrot, revised by Marius Petipa. Orchestra of the Leningrad Theatre of Opera and Ballet, directed by Viktor Fedotov.

HBO Video, color, 1983, 115 minutes.

Since its premiere at the Paris Opéra in 1841, *Giselle* has retained an immense and enduring appeal, and rightly so. Its story is one of love promised, betrayed, redeemed, and lost; its subtext is that of dance itself.

In this traditional production, the Kirov has splendidly captured the nuances of this otherworldly, affecting, and poignant story, due in large part to the marvelously sensitive acting and perfectly controlled dancing of Galina Mezentseva. The joy and childishly innocent delight of her love for Albrecht are stunning, especially compared with the pathos of her "mad scene" and death, and perhaps most of all in the final pas de deux.

Konstantin Zaklinsky makes an extremely handsome and valiant Albrecht. He is deeply engaged in the role, if not terribly individualistic, and handles the important moments competently. The lesser roles are also danced with conviction, especially by Tatyana Terekhova as an icily elegant Myrtha, Queen of the Wilis, and by Olga Vtorushina and Sergei Vuharev, who perform the first-act peasant pas de deux.

The corps performs impeccably in the final act. There are a few unnecessary special effects: Myrtha and Giselle both have to traverse the stage in the air, suspended by wires. The orchestra does well enough, although there's an occasional echo.

The Kirov's proud tradition and disciplined training are evident throughout this performance, which begins with exterior shots of the company's Leningrad home before moving on to the elaborately ornate interior, with its heavily festooned curtain. The oddly lethargic and sparse applause is a distinct distraction, and it is punctuated with strangled cries that may be a Russian form of approval.

Although this may not be the most imaginative performance of *Giselle*, it is a satisfying and often moving rendition.

■ *Giselle*

Music by Adolph Adam, choreography by Alicia Alonso (after the original by Jean Coralli and Jules Perrot). Starring Alicia Alonso, Azari Plisetski, Fernando Alonso, Mirta Plá. Soloists and corps de ballet of the National Ballet of Cuba, National Symphony Orchestra, Manuel Duchesne Cuzán, cond.

VAI, black & white, 1965, 99 minutes.

Alicia Alonso was partially blind at the time this *Giselle* was filmed. It hardly matters—Alonso's interpretation is so enchanting that any flaws fade into the background.

Alonso is a fragile Giselle, right from the start. Her first-act variations are lively and innocent, and what they lack in abandon is more than made up for in style. In her mad scene, when she tears the garland from her neck and falls to the ground, the camera pulls back to show us the whole, sad picture—it is a touching moment. Her second act is less striking, largely because Mirta Plá's Myrtha dominates the stage, but she is impressive nonetheless.

Azari Plisetski's superbly acted and danced Albrecht is both noble and contrite, and his second-act solo is a tour de force. Fernando Alonso's Hyperion is a bit leaden, but his is a strong characterization. Plá's Queen of the Wilis is terrific—sharp, authoritative, and determined. The other soloists and the corps are very good.

Director Enrique Pineda Barnet has arranged for some interesting special effects in the second act—the appearance of the Wilis is eerie and there are some surprises. The editing is not always on target, however. This production is not without its flaws, but Alonso's fans will be more than pleased.

■ *The Little Humpbacked Horse*

Maya Plisetskaya, Vladimir Vasiliev, Alexander Radunsky, Alla Shcherbinina; Corps de Ballet and Orchestra of the Bolshoi Theatre, Algis Zhyuraitis, cond. Music by Rodion Shchedrin, choreography by Alexander Radunsky.

Kultur, 1961, color, 85 minutes.

As far as is known, this ballet has never been mounted in the West, and this tape may therefore be our only chance to see it. It's a worthwhile ballet on a fairy-tale theme and has gone through several incarnations over the years. It debuted in 1864 with music by Pugni and choreography by Arthur Saint-Léon and was rechoreographed in 1895 by Marius Petipa. This version is choreographed as a comedy by the great Russian mime Alexander Radunsky (who also "dances" the role of the dumb, fat Tsar). Unfortunately the effect is somewhat spoiled by Shchedrin's music, which lacks inspiration and the cheerful bounciness that is so wonderfully inherent in the dancing. In all fairness, it is recorded so poorly here that it might actually be more effective in performance than is apparent in this tape.

As usual, Plisetskaya dances brilliantly as the Tsar Maiden and exhibits an unexpected comic sense as well. In the second-act pas de deux, she also performs an intense and focused thirty-two fouettés. As the hero in the guise of a peasant, the athletic Vladimir Vasiliev has more acting than dancing, but he proves himself a master at both.

The costumes and sets were obviously designed with children in mind, but they look garish to an adult eye and are not helped by the peculiar coloring process the Russians were still favoring in the 1960s. Nonetheless, this ballet is a pleasure to watch—for adults as well as kids. Recommended.

■ *The Magic of the Bolshoi Ballet: Performances Legendary in Ballet History Never Previously Seen in the West*

Editors and ballet consultants: Mary Clarke and Clement Crisp; produced in the USSR by Gostelradio.

Home Vision, 1987, black & white and color, 59 minutes.

This tape is a boon for any lover of dance, although its fractured format (over thirty short clips in one hour of running time) makes for only brief glimpses of legendary performers. The good news, of course, is that one never gets bored.

One of the joys on this cassette is Maya Plisetskaya. Never has she been grander, more flamboyant, more unforgettable than she is in the brief bit from *Laurencia* featured here.

Other historical dance revelations include Olga Lepeshinskaya and Pyotr Gusev in two minutes of *Moszkowski Waltz*, filmed in the 1940s. Once again, one is left wanting more. When we are occasionally offered longer excerpts, such as the bedroom pas de deux from *Romeo and Juliet*, danced by Natalia Bessmertnova and Mikhail Lavrovsky, we see surprisingly expressive and sensual dancing; this is true as well of Lyudmila Semenyaka and Alexander Vetrov in the *Blue Bird* pas de deux, despite some awkward partnering by Vetrov.

The real power of this tape lies in its illustration of an underlying theme: tradition counts. What a pity that the excerpts are not twice as long. The tape can be recommended as a compendium and study; as a satisfactory evening at the ballet it doesn't quite make it.

■ *Manon*

Jennifer Penney, Anthony Dowell, David Wall, Derek Rencher, soloists; the Royal Ballet, Orchestra of the Royal Opera House, Covent Garden, Ashley Lawrence, cond. Choreographed and directed by Kenneth MacMillan; directed for TV by Colin Nears.

HBO Video, 1982, color, 113 minutes.

Kenneth MacMillan is one of the great choreographers. His *Manon*, set to music by Jules Massenet, is based on the Abbé Prevost's novel, as is the composer's opera (though the ballet does not use music from the opera). The ballet, a modern lyric masterpiece, is an extended love duet, and both principals here dance with passion and conviction.

Anthony Dowell, as the aristocratic Des Grieux, shows just the right amount of panache mixed with elegance and ably partners Jennifer Penney as Manon, particularly in the two grand pas de deux. His first-act solo is a tour de force of poetic, interpretive dancing, and he is totally believable as the smitten young man. Penney makes a greater impression after the second scene of the first act, where Manon is first tempted by great wealth and loses some of her naiveté; her dancing becomes more assertive and passionate as her character grows worldlier and greedier. Her sickly Manon in the final scene is a truly touching portrayal.

The rest of the cast is first-rate, with special praise reserved for David Wall as the duplicitous Lescaut and David Drew as the jailer; the latter is very effective in the ballet's penultimate scene. Colin Nears's intelligent direction for the small screen allows us to see, for instance, the plotting of Lescaut and Monsieur G.M. with great clarity. If lush story-ballets appeal to you, you'll thoroughly enjoy this one.

Jennifer Penney and Anthony Dowell in the Royal Ballet production of *Manon*. Courtesy HBO Video.

▪ *Martha Graham—Three Contemporary Classics*

Errand into the Maze. Music by Gian Carlo Menotti. Soloists: Terese Capucilli, Larry White. *Cave of the Heart*. Music by Samuel Barber. Soloists: Takako Asakawa, Donlin Foremen, Jacquelyn Bulglisi, Jeanne Ruddy. *Acts of Light*. Music by Carl Nielsen. Soloists: Peggy Lyman, George White, Jr.

VAI, 1984, color, 85 minutes.

Admirers of Martha Graham may want to own this cassette; others may want only to see it once. These performances, though, certainly merit more than a casual viewing, and having Martha Graham herself discussing each work is an added bonus.

Of the three pieces, *Acts of Light* is the least impressive. One of Graham's later works (1981), it is set to music by the Danish composer Carl Nielsen and, as Graham tells us, is about the joy of entering the light after a long period in a dark land. A study in technique brilliantly performed by the sixteen-member company, it leaves one feeling empty and disconcerted.

The remarkable *Cave of the Heart* is very different in tone and choreography. This 1946 dance version of the Medea legend stays in the memory—Takako Asakawa is a stunningly deranged Medea, and Samuel Barber's vibrant music is an integral part of the drama. The small screen actually contributes to our enjoyment of this piece, and director Thomas Grimm deserves special praise. It's a thrilling and chilling performance.

The third work, *Errand into the Maze* (1947), is Graham at her best, demonstrating how modern dance technique can define and amplify emotions.

The orchestral playing is excellent throughout; Herbert Blomstedt conducts the Danish Radio Symphony Orchestra in *Acts of Light* and Jonathan McPhee leads the Aarhus Symphony Orchestra in the other two pieces. These definitive performances are probably essential for Graham fans; others will have to judge for themselves.

▪ *Pas de Deux*

La Sylphide danced by Ghislaine Thesmar and Michael Denard, choreographed by Pierre Lacotte; *Don Quixote* danced by Yoko Morishita and Tetsutaru Shimizu, choreographed by Marius

Petipa; *Le Corsaire* danced by Marielena Mencia and Yanis Pikieris, choreographed by Marius Petipa/Chabukiani; *The Sleeping Beauty* (Act III) danced by Ellen Bauer and Damian Woetzel, choreographed by Marius Petipa; *Flower Festival at Genzano* danced by Linda Hindberg and Arne Villumsen, choreographed by August Bournonville; *Blue Bird* danced by Nadezda Zybine and Luis Astorga, choreographed by Marius Petipa; *Tchaikovsky Pas de Deux* danced by Patricia McBride and Reid Olson, choreographed by George Balanchine.

VAI, color, 1984, 81 minutes.

This tape is best viewed in stages, even by those who always wait impatiently for the soloists to step forward to begin their pas de deux. It's a small example of overkill and, in a way, it's fortunate that the dancing is not spectacular. (That would have been impossible to sit through.) Luckily, of course, the discussion is moot: this is a tape and we can stop and start it where and when we please.

It is interesting to compare techniques here, but one wishes the Bolshoi or the Kirov had been included for even more contrast. As it is, we get Thesmar and Denard from the Paris Opéra ballet in a lovely *Sylphide*, a cool, clean *Quixote* from the Tokyo Ballet's Morishita and Shimizu (the latter a bit earthbound), and a rare look at the great Bournonville's *Flower Festival*, superlatively danced by Hindberg and Villumsen from the very classical Royal Danish Ballet. Less impressive are the Los Angeles Ballet's soloists (Zybine and Astorga) and the Bavarian's *Corsaire* couple. Damian Woetzel does well in *Sleeping Beauty*, especially when one realizes that he was only seventeen at the time.

John Clifford, artistic director of the Los Angeles Ballet, is our informative and charming host. As one might gather, this is not a thrill a minute but, rather, an absorbing look at what is normally the high point of any ballet evening.

■ *Raymonda*

Ludmila Semenyaka, Erek Moukhamedov, Gedeminas Taranda. Music by Alexander Glazunov. Choreography by Yuri Grigorovich and Marius Petipa.

Kultur, color, 1982, 146 minutes.

Ask any group of balletomanes if they can explain the plot of *Raymonda*, and you will invariably have an argument on your hands. It's a rare performance that is less than confusing. This one, although it does have its enjoyable moments, doesn't get close.

The labyrinthine plot involves passions among thirteenth-century Crusaders and Saracens, and Glazunov's score reflects the turbulence and murkiness of the action. Petipa's original choreography is always being "improved," and Grigorovich here attempts to do the same. In this performance it's hard to tell where Petipa ends and Grigorovich takes over— a good sign—but the ballet still remains oddly truncated and confusing, despite some grand dancing by the three leads.

Moukhamedov is a major dancer in his prime, and Semenyaka is lithe and attractive. Taranda is interesting, but much of his work here seems pointless. The corps has plenty to do, but their part in the story seems superfluous and adds to the confusion.

If you must see *Raymonda*, then get this version—for the simple reason that it's the only tape of the ballet extant. Enjoy it if you can.

■ *Romeo and Juliet*

Alessandra Ferri, Wayne Eagling, David Drew, Mark Freeman. The Royal Ballet, Orchestra of the Royal Opera House, Covent Garden; Ashley Lawrence, cond. Directed by Colin Nears and Kenneth MacMillan.

HBO Video, color, 1984, 128 minutes.

This is Kenneth MacMillan's 1965 version of Shakespeare's tragedy, set to the music of Sergei Prokofiev. It has stood up quite well.

Any choreographer faces severe difficulties with this ballet, as the music is impossibly literal and grandiose. There is no way around it, for Prokofiev has in effect written a script, not a score. MacMillan's choreography does well by the score, but as there is so much need for mime, the dancing itself is perforce extremely limited. There is more spectacle than ballet; large, boisterous masses of dancers throng the stage, rendering a vision of a rich and overcrowded Verona.

Nicholas Georgiadis has provided an ornate High Renaissance setting. In this performance everyone is hugely overdressed, except for the two lovers, and occasionally the stage seems hardly large enough to contain the whirling trains and swinging cloaks. But it is indeed grand, and the lavishness of scenery, sets, and costumes is impressive.

The real reason to pay attention to this video is the young Alessandra Ferri, who has appeared in this country and garnered great praise. Her Juliet is childlike in her fragility, and she looks the part to perfection in an adolescently luminous way. Her line is good, her dancing lyrical, delicately correct, and striking; and yet there is something not quite fully formed about her. She doesn't convince us of the depth of her feelings. It is hard for any dancer not basically an actress to make much impression in this ballet; Ferri is more ballerina than actress.

Wayne Eagling, as Romeo, is competent but not commanding as a romantic dancer. His approach is nonchalant, sketchy, and pleasant but not affecting in the way Anthony Dowell managed to be in the part, and certainly no match for Nureyev in the 1966 film from Kultur. He has some stirring series of steps and some extended *chaîné* turns (which he does well), but overall, it is not an inspiring role for him.

Still, if a full-length version of this unwieldy but at times exciting ballet is wanted, this one is grand, and chock-full of action. And the pounding music and story never fail to move.

Alessandra Ferri and Wayne Eagling in the Royal Ballet production of *Romeo and Juliet*. Courtesy HBO Video.

■ *Romeo and Juliet*

Rudolf Nureyev, Margot Fonteyn, Julia Farron, David Blair, Michael Somes, Desmond Doyle, Anthony Dowell. Music by Sergei Prokofiev; choreography by Kenneth MacMillan. The Royal Ballet, Orchestra of the Royal Opera House, Covent Garden, John Lanchbery, cond. Produced and directed by Paul Czinner.

Kultur, color, 1966, 124 minutes.

Here we have the young Nureyev at his most coltish, the mature Fonteyn at her most thoughtful and graceful, the Royal Ballet in top form, Kenneth MacMillan's passionately involving choreography, and some fine photography. What more could one ask for?

This is a very special film. Much like Paul Czinner's *Der Rosenkavalier*, the production evokes an era long gone and captures it on film. We see Rudolf Nureyev, just five years after his defection to the West, dancing with an extraordinary, exuberant certainty that comes just once in a lifetime. And here is the porcelain figure of Fonteyn, pensive but light as a feather. When Nureyev lifts her there are moments when it looks as if she might float away.

To these spectacular central performances are added those of the splendid Julia Farron and Michael Somes as Lady Capulet and Capulet, with assistance from a superb David Blair as Mercutio and Desmond Doyle as Tybalt; there's not a weak link in the cast. Nicholas Georgiadis' striking sets and costumes add to the effect. Some might prefer Lavrovsky's choreography, particularly in the balcony scene, but there are many wonderful moments in MacMillan's, not least his handling of the corps de ballet. (Lavrovsky's—with Ulanova, no less—is available on Kultur.)

This magnificent production is highly recommended to all lovers of great dancing.

■ *Romeo and Juliet*

Rudolf Nureyev, Carla Fracci, Margot Fonteyn, Bruno Telloli, Bruno Vescova, Elettra Morini; Corps de ballet and orchestra of La Scala, Milan, Michel Sasson, cond. Music by Sergei Prokofiev, choreography by Rudolf Nureyev.

Kultur, color, 1982, 129 minutes.

This tape promises more than it actually delivers. Nureyev has choreographed this great work for an Italian audience, and he seems to have incorporated a great deal of Italian street body language into the crowd scenes. It doesn't always work, and the effort often seems oddly strained. On the plus side, we see Romeo's motives more clearly than usual—he's not only smitten by love for Juliet but also has a conscience.

Both Nureyev and Fracci were in their forties when this was taped in 1982; Fracci looks fresh and beautiful, and her Juliet is a great success. Fonteyn is Lady Capulet, and her formidable acting talent enables her to shine where others in this role merely appear. (Nureyev is very kind to her in this staging of the ballet.) Nureyev's Romeo is uneven: at moments he is truly inspired and seems to be in his twenties again; at other moments one can see the effort. The cast, in general, performs well, with a special nod of approval to Bruno Vescova's Mercutio and Elettra Morini's Nurse. The corps is excellent.

The quality of the tape is first-rate, and conductor Sasson leads the La Scala forces handsomely. This is a cassette for Fonteyn, Fracci, and Nureyev fans and for those curious to see Nureyev's way with a modern classic. One may prefer to stick with the Kultur performance of Lavrovsky's choreography starring Ulanova, although Nureyev's isn't wholly dismissable. It just isn't a very interesting version.

■ *Romeo and Juliet*

Music by Sergei Prokofiev, choreography by Leonid Lavrovsky. Galina Ulanova, Yuri Zhdanov, Sergei Koren, Alexei Yermolayev, Alexander Radunsky, other soloists; Bolshoi Ballet, Orchestra of the Bolshoi Theatre, Gennady Rozhdestvensky, cond. Directed by Leonid Lavrovsky and Lev Arnshtam.

Kultur, color, 1954, 95 minutes.

Despite some vaguely surreal color (the Soviet processing was always a problem) and some bumpy editing, this classic film is a must for any ballet fan's video library. The role was created for Ulanova, and here she is in all her glory. About fifty minutes of the score have been excised to reduce it to this manageable length, but only die-hard purists will object. The only upsetting cut is in the balcony scene—a few minutes are gone—but otherwise all of Juliet's role is included.

This is a well-staged action drama, handsomely filmed both indoors and out, with plenty of swordplay. Superb in Leonid Lavrovsky's heart-stopping choreography, the mature Ulanova is a perfect girlish Juliet without being coy. We feel her shyness, we feel the girl becoming aware of herself as a woman, and her intense humanity is in every step. When she and Romeo meet, it is clearly love at first sight; Yuri Zhdanov's ardent, caring performance is a jewel as well. The balcony scene, performed on a black stage with some cinematic superimpositions, is touching and delicate. Ulanova's troubled solo before she gets the philter is superb.

The supporting cast is excellent, with special praise going to that consummate character ballet dancer, Alexander Radunsky, who plays a most convincing Capulet.

Rozhdestvensky is a sympathetic conductor, and the sound has been remastered. This is a historical document and a wonderfully pleasing one at that.

■ *The Royal Ballet*

Margot Fonteyn, Michael Somes, Julia Farron; the Royal Ballet, Orchestra of the Royal Opera House, Covent Garden. Produced and directed by Paul Czinner. *Swan Lake* (Act II), *The Firebird*, *Ondine*.

Paramount Home Video, color, 1959, 132 minutes.

This generous tape captures Margot Fonteyn in her prime. Producer-director Paul Czinner has done a splendid job, using as many as forty-four cameras to capture the action, and the result is impressive. These scenes were taken from actual performances at Covent Garden; none were specially staged. Aside from the fact that the dancers occasionally dance themselves out of a frame and that the color in this thirty-year-old film is peculiar, this tape is highly recommended.

The twenty minutes of *Swan Lake* included here are wonderful. Fonteyn is a girlish Odette with expressive face and graceful body, Michael Somes partners her well if without much real individual character, and the corps is fine. *The Firebird* is another story. Coming as it does after Fonteyn's lyrical Odette, it is an amazing demonstration of her energy and versatility. She dances with a vengeance, hurling herself around almost dangerously. At times she actually looks as if she's speaking, so startling and totally effective is her body's vocabulary. Somes is an excellent Prince Ivan and looks very comfortable with folk dance idiom. Franklin White is suitably evil as the wizard.

Ondine was created for Fonteyn in 1958 by Frederick Ashton, to music by Hans Werner Henze. It is an overly dramatic work, full of conflict and intrigue. Henze's score is fascinating, if not always entirely approachable, and Ashton's eponymous water sprite is another of his memorable characters. Appropriately, Fonteyn dances here with great fluidity. She is all surprise and delicacy, and when she sees her shadow (the Prince plays a shadow-dance game with her) the effect is magical. The pas de deux before the Act I wedding scene is one of Ashton's best, and the second act gives Julia Farron a chance to dance brilliantly as the jealous Berta. In the third act Czinner takes full advantage of the medium of film: here Fonteyn as Ondine is seen literally floating in air. The work's sudden ending, in which Ondine kisses the Prince (a passionate Somes) and he dies on the spot, is moving if a bit abrupt. All in all, although *Ondine* has its *longueurs*, it is definitely worth seeing.

Fans of Fonteyn will want this movie; others could probably do with more of *Swan Lake*. The color is generally garish, but the production values are otherwise high.

■ *Spartacus*

Vladimir Vasiliev, Natalia Bessmertnova, Maris Liepa, Nina Timofeyeva; corps de ballet, orchestra, and chorus of the Bolshoi Theatre, Algis Zhyuraitis, cond. Music by Aram Khachaturian, choreography by Yuri Grigorovich.

Kultur, color, 1977, 95 minutes.

■ *Spartacus*

Erek Moukhamedov, Natalia Bessmertnova, Mikhail Gabovich, Maria Bylova; corps de ballet, orchestra, and chorus of the Bolshoi Theatre, Algis Zhyuraitis, cond. Music by Aram Khachaturian, choreography by Yuri Grigorovich.

HBO Video, color, 1984, 128 minutes.

This relatively new ballet about the slave Spartacus, who revolted against the Romans and their general, Crassus, has had a checkered past. It was first produced at the Kirov in 1956 with choreography by Leonid Jacobson, but both critics and public agreed that it was seriously lacking in depth. Two years later Igor Moiseyev reworked it, and it was presented at the Bolshoi. The ballet still did not please. In 1968, Yuri Grigorovich, the Bolshoi's director, tried his hand at it. It was an immediate success and has remained a favorite ever since.

Cinematic in scope, it is more of a spectacle than a classical ballet, and it never bores; the action is incessant and unrelenting. *Spartacus* is also the least "feminine" of all repertory ballets—some call it a poem to machismo.

The music by Aram Khachaturian is noisy and full of brass and percussion. Natalia Bessmertnova dances the role of Phrygia, Spartacus' lover, in both performances. In the earlier Kultur film, she is more impulsive and energetic, and her technique is beyond reproach. In the live Bolshoi performance, taped seven years later, there is no significant diminution of her technique, but her smoothness and seriousness in the sadder, more tender moments add a depth not found in the earlier version. As the conniving and ambitious Aegina, Maria Bylova wins out over Nina Timofeyeva. It is all too easy to see this role as the stereotypical nasty vamp, but Bylova does more. Her Aegina is dangerous, sensuous, and powerful; her dancing is stunning and provocative. Timofeyeva is a superb technician, but Bylova brings an edge to the part that puts the ballet into perspective and helps define the difficult character of Crassus.

Crassus is a cruel coward. Maris Liepa in the Kultur tape steals the show (he originated the part). He plays him as ice-cold and rigid, but his dancing has great energy and verve. Gabovich, on HBO, is a good actor but lacks elevation. His strutting manner makes a point, but Liepa draws the fuller portrait.

In the crucial title role, we have two great dancers on both tapes. The role was created for Vasiliev, and he is a powerhouse. His turns, elevation, and one-arm lifts are a testament to the strengths of the great Russian dancers. But he can also be tender, both in his pas de deux with Bessmertnova and in his interior "monologues." Almost, but not quite in his league is the intense Erek Moukhamedov, who clearly realizes that what he does with his face is as important as what he does with his body. He seems to get stronger as the ballet progresses, and his dancing before the final battle is almost superhuman. The corps is equally good in both versions.

The Kultur version cuts about a half hour of the music. Made on a sound stage, it is full of such cinematic tricks as superimpositions, split screens, slow-motion shots, and close-ups. The HBO tape, on the other hand, is of a live performance at the Bolshoi—without any gimmicks, offering a complete score and welcome audience reaction. In this tape TV

Vladimir Vasiliev and Natalia Bessmertnova in the Bolshoi Ballet production of *Spartacus*. Courtesy Kultur Video.

director Preben Montell has done a superb job in allowing us to see everything from just the right angle.

The Kultur print is excellent, with a black band at top and bottom (a sort of CinemaScopic effect); and while the HBO picture is a bit grainy, it isn't a problem. HBO's sound is also better.

The costumes and scenery of both productions are essentially the same—lush and spectacular. These two tapes *are* very different experiences. The immediacy of the live performance is as enthralling as the professional moviemaking of the other. Try to see both.

■ Stars of the Russian Ballet

Maya Plisetskaya, Galina Ulanova, Pyotr Gusev, Natalia Dudinskaya, Konstantin Sergeyev, Vakhtang Chabukiani, others; Orchestra of the Leningrad Theatre, V. Dubovskly and P. Felot, conductors. Excerpts from *Swan Lake, The Fountain of Bakhchisarai, The Flames of Paris*.

Kultur, color, 1953, 80 minutes.

This is an odd but essential tape for any serious collection. The selections from *Swan Lake* alone are valuable insofar as they are the only extant footage of the great Ulanova as Odette. Ulanova was forty-three when this was filmed, but her remarkable technique, great warmth, and eloquent movement were undiminished—one can only regret that much of Odette's role is cut and that she was not dancing Odile as well. Natalia Dudinskaya takes that role, and good though she is, she could never be mistaken for Ulanova. Sergeyev, who was artistic director of the Kirov at the time, is a bulky dancer who nonetheless can lighten his approach when necessary. Unfortunately, the Russians, in an attempt at modernism, have mixed animation with real stage sets and the effect is maddening. Apart from that, it's worth seeing.

The second set of excerpts is from *The Fountain of Bakhchisarai*, choreographed by Rostislav Zakharov. Its improbable plot takes place in a harem and seems to be about the Khan's past and present concubines. Ulanova is the new girl and Plisetskaya is the former favorite. This is the only time the two were filmed onstage together, so it gives ballet fans a chance to see their sharply different techniques. Ulanova's poise, delicacy, and innocence are a perfect foil to Plisetskaya's tempestuous virtuosity. Plisetskaya dances with an almost abnormal intensity, and where she offers thrills, Ulanova offers calm lyricism. Pyotr Gusev as the Khan is spectacularly energetic and expressive, almost making us forget the outlandishness of the production.

The final ballet is of interest to fans of the swashbuckling Chabukiani, who in 1934 was the first Soviet male dancer to tour the United States. The ballet itself is about the French Revolution and relies heavily on the corps, who dance splendidly. The music is a hodgepodge of tunes from French composers arranged by Boris Asafiev, and an unnamed chorus intones in the background. This 1932 ballet was a success in the Soviet Union for obvious political reasons; we can only be glad that it was abridged for this presentation.

The color throughout this release is garish and makes everything look amazingly tawdry—another Soviet experiment that didn't quite work. But don't let that, or the animation, dissuade you from buying or renting this tape; it's a dance history lesson and a fascinating evening of ballet rolled into one.

■ *Swan Lake*

Natalia Makarova and Anthony Dowell with the Royal Ballet; Orchestra of the Royal Ballet. Directed by John Michael Phillips. Produced by Thames Television Production in association with Covent Garden Video Productions Limited.

HBO Video, color, 1980, 137 minutes.

This is the ballet of all ballets; *Swan Lake* is the grandest, most haunting, and yet most elusive of the great nineteenth-century classical ballets. Tchaikovsky's fabulous music is filled with color and excitement, swiftly changing moods, and soaring melodies.

This performance was recorded live at Covent Garden. The sets and costumes by Leslie Hurry look a bit faded, with custardy colors and fussy details, and the costumes for the national dances of the third act (the Spanish, Neapolitan, Hungarian, and Polish variations) are, with few exceptions, downright ugly. Nevertheless, it is the kind of ambitious production that *Swan Lake* demands, and the two stars make it all worthwhile.

Anthony Dowell is one of the more sensitive romantic dancers of our time, and he has the ability to perform the most difficult turns, leaps, and lifts, not only with grace and ease but with a kind of confident modesty. He seems to have no need to knock us out with his personality or daring; he projects himself comfortably, but still deeply, through the character he portrays. A more responsive cavalier to the glittering, many-sided Makarova couldn't be imagined.

As for Makarova, her dancing is mesmerizing. Her extensions, port de bras, the arch of the back, and the superb pointe work are her very own, but she creates a thoroughly convincing portrait of the Swan Queen—regal yet vulnerable, poignant in her slow progression from fear to trust in the Prince. Her Odile is technically strong, while the characterization remains a bit aloof, not quite as realized as that of the tender Odette.

The choreography is that of Petipa-Ivanov, with additional interpolations by Frederick Ashton and with a first-act solo for Prince Siegfried choreographed by Rudolph Nureyev. The corps of swans dances creditably, but the dancing of various soloists is not as sharp as one might want. The British tendency toward emotional stiffness and a cool demeanor is not enough of a problem to destroy the value of this video, which is rightfully centered in the thrilling work of the two principal dancers. Recommended.

■ Swan Lake

Maya Plisetskaya, Nikolai Fadeyechev, Vladimir Levashev, V. Khomyakov, soloists; the Bolshoi Ballet; Orchestra of the Bolshoi Theatre, Moscow.

Kultur, color, 1957, 81 minutes.

This best known of all classical ballets is served up superbly in this somewhat frustrating film (the director frequently cuts away from the action onstage, even in the middle of the two great pas de deux). Still, just having the young Plisetskaya's Odile and Odette on tape is a treat, especially since it was this ballet that made her reputation as Ulanova's successor as the Bolshoi's prima ballerina. It is also easy to see why she has been compared to Maria Callas: the raw emotionalism of her dancing is similar to that great diva's singing style. In many ways her Odile is preferable to her Odette: she is the perfect evil seductress.

Nikolai Fadeyechev is a handsome, manly Prince and dances with great flair, and the Bolshoi corps lives up to its reputation. The filming is a bit overdone; the many shots of lobbies, dressing rooms, and audience soon pall, and in addition, some of the long shots are often unclear. But no ballet fan should be without Plisetskaya's Swan Lake.

Dance: Documentaries and Movies

■ *Bold Steps: A Portrait of the National Ballet of Canada*

Directed by Cyril Frankel.

Home Vision, color, 1986, 81 minutes.

This documentary, made to commemorate the National Ballet of Canada's thirty-five years of existence, is a high-spirited, entertaining look at a youthful and talented company. There are interviews with Erik Bruhn, the former artistic director, and Celia Franca, its founder, as well as brief chats with Rudolf Nureyev and Mikhail Baryshnikov and various members of the company, past and present.

In its early, desperate days, the company toured Canada performing one-night stands—often in barns, hockey arenas, and gyms—battling storms and economic deficits. Nureyev's production of *Sleeping Beauty* finally put it on the map as a significant international company, and although the production was a financial disaster, it gave the company a direct link to the Russian traditions that Nureyev represented. Nureyev is seen rehearsing with Karen Kain, while Baryshnikov is shown rehearsing with the dancers before his appearance with the company at its 1984 gala.

Bruhn and Franca discuss the balletic traditions they attempted to develop, with Bruhn commenting on the great depth of talent he found when he took over at a time of artistic and economic difficulty. Betty Oliphant's work with the company's school is featured, and there are charming glimpses of the school's scouts auditioning young children in a nationwide talent hunt. The company tries not only to prepare its students for careers in dance but also to maintain high academic standards for those whose lives will not be given over completely to the ballet stage.

Quite a bit of dance is shown too, even though this is essentially a profile of a company. Yoko Ichino and the remarkable Kevin Pugh are shown in rehearsal and in performance of the pas de deux from *Don Quixote*. These scenes alone are worth the price of admission: Pugh's amazing talents are displayed in some truly exciting footwork. The same can be said for Owen Montague in a scene from *Oiseaux Exotiques*.

Excerpts from both classical and contemporary dance are offered, including *Swan Lake*, Makarova's *La Bayadère*, Glenn Tetley's *Sphinx*, Harald Lander's *Etudes*, and Erik Bruhn's *Here We Come* to the music of Morton Gould. All of these demonstrate the company's wide talent and young energy. Though perhaps not an essential addition to a dance fan's library, this is still a very enjoyable look at the on- and offstage personality of an expanding international ballet company.

■ Fernando Bujones: *In His Own Image*

Kultur, color, 1980, 57 minutes.

No one can doubt the stature of Fernando Bujones in the world of ballet—he is one of the best. This self-serving video presents him in nine ballet variations and pas de deux with companies in New York, Tokyo, Puerto Rico, and Rio de Janeiro. His virtuosity is evident, and if the dancing itself isn't enough to prove it, we also get testimonials from Robert Denvers, Cynthia Gregory, Jane Herman, and others, who tell us again and again how grand Bujones is. These promotional statements are a bore—skip them, or just turn the sound off.

But the dancing is well worth it all. Bujones has a great technique and an uncanny ability to appear suspended in midair when he leaps. We see him in *Le Corsaire, Raymonda, Don Quixote, Swan Lake, Giselle,* and other ballets.

Producer-director Zeida Cecilia-Mendez has chosen her excerpts well. Too bad she didn't allow the dancing to speak for itself.

■ *The Children of Theatre Street*

With Princess Grace of Monaco; an Earle Mack film directed by Robert Dornhelm.

Kultur, color, 1978, 92 minutes.

This unusual, worthwhile film was made in Leningrad at the school of the Kirov Ballet, perhaps the world's greatest training ground for superb dancers. It follows students from the time they enter the school all the way to their graduation performance, and offers a rare glimpse into a competitive and often disappointing world.

Though the film is a documentary, producer Mack and director Dornhelm have attempted to provide a plotline by concentrating on three students: a ten-year-old girl, her boyfriend, and the girl's godmother, who is a senior at the school. The plot is sketchy and hardly holds up, and though Dornhelm is a fine director (this film was nominated for an Academy Award), he keeps the film almost too busy, interspersing shots of Leningrad with the history, daily life, and rigors of the school.

The film opens in Monte Carlo's exquisite opera house. The late Princess Grace is a sweet and informative narrator, if lacking in energy. The cinematography is excellent, although the color is a bit less vibrant than one might want.

If you're eager to see the workings of the Russian balletic tradition and training, this film will hold your interest. It's an entertaining and informative show.

■ Fonteyn and Nureyev: *The Perfect Partnership*

Margot Fonteyn, Rudolf Nureyev. Produced and directed by Peter Batty.

Kultur, black & white and color, 1985, 90 minutes.

This tape is a record of a unique dance partnership and offers a fascinating look at the young, vibrant Nureyev. Since he first burst onto the international ballet scene, his dancing has often taken a backseat to legends of his defection, arrogance, and offstage exploits. This film tells a more balanced story. And those who admire Margot Fonteyn will appreciate the extensive footage on this great British dancer.

It's easy to see why the role of the male dancer in classic ballet—essentially the dignified partner of the prima ballerina—was changed forever when Nureyev stepped onstage. His astonishing virtuosity, sensuous and considerate partnering, and vitality are a pleasure to behold.

Fonteyn herself seems more feminine, more passionately involved when in Nureyev's presence. Always a superb technician, she dances here with a wistfulness and yearning not commonly seen in previous performances.

They appear in *Les Sylphides* and *Le Corsaire* plus extended excerpts, filmed in 1963, from Ashton's *Marguerite and Armand* (created especially for them), and in the balcony scene from *Romeo and Juliet*. Nureyev's energy is matched by Fonteyn's sweetness and delicacy; perhaps his incandescence, contrasted with her cool precision, proved the winning combination.

There's plenty about their personal lives on this tape, but it's the dancing that counts. Any ballet fan without this tape is missing a crucial period in the history of dance—and an evening of great entertainment. Highly recommended.

■ Godunov: *The World to Dance In*

With Alexander Godunov.

Kultur, color, 1983, 60 minutes.

"Sasha" Godunov defected to the West while on tour with the Bolshoi Ballet in 1979 in New York, but he has yet to find his place in the ballet scene. Not that he isn't popular, as this documentary never fails to indicate. His imposing 6'1" figure has made Maya Plisetskaya, Cynthia Gregory, and Natalia Makarova enthusiastic over his partnering. With his straggling, shoulder-length blond hair, pouting lips, and sultry, smoky eyes, he is the very picture of the romantic hero.

After early years with the Moiseyev Dance Troupe, Godunov was taken on by the Bolshoi Ballet in 1973, a protégé of Yuri Grigorovich and Alexei Yermolayev. He immediately became a soloist with the company and was selected by Plisetskaya to be her partner. We get a glimpse of a very exciting *Anna Karenina* pas de deux filmed with (and choreographed by) the great Russian ballerina in 1974. But the excitement and energy of this clip are hardly matched by the rest of the dancing, most of which consists of Godunov in the bravura variations from Petipa's *Le Corsaire*, which are repeated endlessly throughout.

Shortly after his defection, Godunov signed on with the American Ballet Theatre, specializing in the classical roles of Russian ballet. In a charming interview in the rehearsal studio with Cynthia Gregory, their partnership is briefly described. The enigma of Godunov is that while he never fails to bring audiences to their feet with the speed of his turns, the power of his leaps, and the virility of his approach, his characterizations seem curiously lacking in expressiveness. We see him signing autographs, getting on and off airplanes, walking through airports, taking hotel elevators, appearing at a ballet class for teenage girls: "Okay, girls, work hard!"

Less about dance than about a media star, *Godunov: The World to Dance In* is recommended only as a piece of engaging fluff.

◼ Peter Martins: *A Dancer*

Directed by Jorgen Leth.

Kultur, color, 1978, 54 minutes.

This is a no-nonsense Danish view of one of the best dancers of the past two decades. Peter Martins was trained and danced with the Royal Danish Ballet before coming to the New York City Ballet and George Balanchine in 1969.

Attractive and charming, Martins is a serious artist and a strenuous critic of himself. Though seemingly self-assured, he is driven by a fierce desire for improvement—for "exploring the possibilities of being a dancer"—and seems to grow bored once the challenge has been met. These qualities are much in evidence in this commendable documentary, which wastes no time on glamour, romance, or jet-set gossip.

Instead, we are given a picture of the toil and sweat that working in dance at the top requires—the hours of class, rehearsal, and exercise, the painstaking attention to detail, to gesture, to makeup, to costume. Stanley Williams, a gifted teacher with the School of American Ballet, is shown in several close-up segments working intensely with Martins on his technique.

Excerpts from Balanchine's *Agon* and from *Chaconne*, both danced by Martins with Suzanne Farrell, enable us to appreciate the beauty and elegance of their partnership. Martins is also shown as choreographer, working with Heather Watts and Daniel Duell on his first ballet, *Calcium Light Night*. Martins' determination to extract the best from himself, his humor, his delicacy as a heroic dancer and partner, are all explored here. The camerawork is solid, the sound fine, the script deft and unobtrusive. Highly recommended.

■ Natasha: *A Dance Entertainment*

Natalia Makarova. With Anthony Dowell, Denys Ganio, Gary Chryst, Tim Flavin, and the Norman Maen Dancers. Produced by Julia Matheson. Directed by Derek Bailey.

Kultur, color, 1985, 70 minutes.

In addition to being terrific "entertainment," *Natasha* offers superb dance. From the moment its star, Natalia Makarova, whirls onto the screen in a brilliant yellow costume, the viewer falls under her spell.

Each excerpt of dance is introduced by Makarova. As in all the segments, the ballets are sensitively staged. The only misstep is the presence of an apparently small audience, whose apparent reserve makes the applause seem slender and apologetic. The quality of the sound, featuring the Royal Philharmonic, is good, and for the most part, the camerawork is steady and intelligent.

To show Makarova's great range, two excerpts from Broadway shows are used: the wonderfully comic seduction scene from *On Your Toes*, for which she won a Tony Award in 1983, and an excerpt from *Natasha* with the Norman Maen Dancers.

An amusing rendition of "Begin the Beguine," danced with Gary Chryst, with choreography by Peter Gennaro, is a sort of elegant Apache-style number, hot and sensuous, yet lighthearted.

Back in the standard ballet arena, an excerpt from Roland Petit's once scandalous *Carmen* is performed with Denys Ganio, a strong-faced Mediterranean-looking dancer. Makarova's back extension and the strength and suppleness of her body are remarkable. She is always inside the character, completely concentrated, yet passionate, occasionally willful and extravagant.

Manon pairs Dowell with Makarova in a romantic and vibrant love duet from Kenneth MacMillan's ballet. Dowell's sensitive partnering is a pleasure, his abandonment to the role and his response to his ballerina finely developed. The classical repertory is not forgotten: *The Dying Swan* (Fokine) and *La Sylphide* are both included. Her great skill as a dramatic dancer is felt here, too.

In short, as a portrait of a charming and exotic professional, this is not only entertainment, but also a dance video of merit.

■ **Pavlova:** *A Tribute to the Legendary Ballerina*

Directed by Pierre Morin. Produced by Société Radio-Canada of Montreal and Premiere Performance Corporation.

Sony, color, 1983, 81 minutes.

The name Pavlova is legendary in ballet and a tempting subject for a video résumé of a career that by all standards was a fabulous one in terms of achievement and international fame (she traveled over 350,000 miles on tours from 1910 to 1931).

Yet, how—even remotely—to capture the spirit of her dancing? Pretty near impossible, and this tape does not get close. The narration is delivered by Leslie Caron, and the dancing is provided by a collection of famous and not-so-famous dancers.

Throughout, the use of tricky effects, fade-ins, fade-outs, odd angles, fuzzy focus, wind machines to lift the gauzy skirts, and the rather strange use of outdoor sets, serve not to illuminate the art of Anna Pavlova but to show off the techniques of latter-day TV art. Excerpts of Pavlova's most famous ballets are presented, with Valentina Kozlova and Patrick Bissell performing the third-act pas de deux from *Don Quixote*, Jolinda Menendez valiantly attempting Nadine Legat's highly romantic *La Nuit*, and the pièce de résistance, *The Dying Swan*. It isn't that the dancers here are inadequate, but they seem inappropriate. Why not include film clips of Pavlova herself dancing?

We also see Ronald Reagan, of all people, dancing with Ann Marie De Angelo in an elaborate cinematic set with water rushing over rocks, mists rising around the dancers' feet, clouds wafting on- and offstage—this is *The Awakening of Flora*, but one has to wonder what it all has to do with Pavlova.

In between the excerpts, Caron offers facts about Pavlova, using still photos, snapshots, playbills, and posters. There is also a very brief bit from Pavlova's only venture into full-length moving pictures, *The Dumb Girl of Portici*.

This program is a mess, and despite some talented performers (especially Marianna Tcherkassky) and the constant allure of the name Pavlova, too much of the essential Anna is just not here.

■ *A Portrait of Giselle*

Directed by Muriel Balash, conceived and produced by Joseph Wishy. Hosted and narrated by Anton Dolin. With Alicia Alonso, Yvette Chauviré, Carla Fracci, Tamara Karsavina, Natalia Makarova, Alicia Markova, Olga Spessivtzeva, Galina Ulanova, Patricia McBride, and Helgi Tomasson.

Kultur, black & white and color, 1982, 97 minutes.

In this informative and entertaining film, Anton Dolin, himself once a fine Albrecht and choreographer, acts as host and narrator. He tells us of *Giselle*'s beginnings, instructs Patricia McBride and Helgi Tomasson in its nuances, introduces us to filmed footage of the ballet, and interviews eight great Giselles of the past and present.

Natalia Makarova, seen in the first-act solo, is brilliant, as is Spessivtzeva. Carla Fracci's excerpts prove that the praise for this consummate actress/dancer is well deserved. Alicia Alonso talks about her first *Giselle* in 1943, and the great Ulanova offers her insights. Alicia Markova is seen dancing with Dolin; Yvette Chauviré also contributes her thoughts on the role. The brief interview with the very elderly Tamara Karsavina is less than informative, unfortunately.

By the close of this tape, we are closer to understanding the nature of this great classic ballet than ever before. Recommended.

■ *Romantic Era: The Beauty of an Age Captured by Four Legends of Dance*

Alicia Alonso, Carla Fracci, Ghislaine Thesmar, Eva Evdokimova.

Kultur, color, 1980, 89 minutes.

As Anton Dolin tells us in this fine documentary, for many years he has owned a famous nineteenth-century lithograph of four great ballerinas as they appeared together in the *Pas de Quatre* in 1845 in London. The four epitomized the sudden flowering of the romantic era in ballet, when the role of women became the dominant feature of dance, helped in part by the invention of the strengthened toe shoe. The four were Marie Taglioni (the first woman to dance *en pointe*), Carlotta Grisi, Lucile Grahn, and Fanny Cerrito.

In the 1930s Dolin decided to recreate the *Pas de Quatre;* after much research and the discovery of the original music, he choreographed the work in 1941. In the current film, the four "greats" are Alicia Alonso of the Ballet Nacional de Cuba, Carla Fracci of La Scala, Ghislaine Thesmar of the Paris Opéra Ballet, and Eva Evdokimova of the Berlin Opera Ballet. They appear in a program performed at the eighth annual International Cervantes Festival of the Arts in Guanajuato, Mexico, and were taped live for this video.

This very satisfying film offers a charming taste of what the romantic ballet (roughly 1830–1860) was all about. As Erik Bruhn says, in a script by Faubion Bowers, it was an era of belief in wilis, spirits, dead souls returned to life, of fantastic imaginary happenings. It was also a time of a particular style of dance, a style that the four ballerinas in the film discuss together.

The film consists mainly of dancing interspersed with brief segments from the dancers' discussion. Each ballerina appears with her partner in a separate pas de deux rechoreographed from an original nineteenth-century ballet. The first, *Esmeralda,* features Eva Evdokimova with the lyrical and exciting Peter Schaufuss. The Bournonville training of both dancers is evident in their technique, with its natural grace, exuberance, speed, and fluent movement, and in the integration of mime into the dance itself.

We next see Ghislaine Thesmar and Michael Denard of the Paris Opéra Ballet in *Nathalie, or the Swiss Milkmaid.* A young girl falls in love with a statue and is horrified when it comes to life before her. Happily, the cavalier is enchanted with her, and they dance with peasantlike joie de vivre into a rosy future. Denard's technique is impeccable, and Thesmar may be one of the most elegant of all the ballerinas presented.

In Carla Fracci's pas de deux with the outclassed James Urbain, her vibrant personality dominates in the story of *La Péri,* in which a Persian courtesan appears in a drug-induced hallucination to seduce the dreamer. Fracci's style is extroverted, supremely self-confident, only occasionally moving, but authoritative.

The amazing Alicia Alonso gives us an exquisitely pure, classically fine rendition of the pas de deux from *Robert le Diable,* with a stalwart and sympathetic Jorge Esquivel, her partner since about 1974. Hers is a somewhat mannered presentation but thoroughly that of a prima ballerina assoluta.

The four ballerinas do the adagio from the second act of *Giselle* and then, the pièce de résistance, the *Pas de Quatre,* a beautiful and funny portrayal of the ever so delicate, refined gracefulness of the romantic ballerina, multiplied to the fourth power. The ladies play it for grace, charm, and satire.

A most enjoyable film that presents a coherent and lovely look at some fine dancers, set in the historical context of the balletic tradition. Recommended.

Dance: Special Films

■ *The Ballerinas*

Carla Fracci, Peter Ustinov.

Kultur, color, 1987, two segments, each 54 minutes.

Made by Polish TV, with a script by Domenico de Martini, this video is, quite unintentionally, a barrel of laughs. The star is Carla Fracci, here playing some of the legendary ballerinas of the golden era of ballet in Paris: Maria Taglioni, Carlotta Grisi, Anna Pavlova, Fanny Elssler, Tamara Karsavina, Emma Livry, Olga Spessivtzeva, and others. Fracci's partners are not without fame themselves: Vladimir Vasiliev, Peter Schaufuss, Michael Denard, Richard Cragun, Stephen Jeffries, Charles Jude, and Juan Antonio. And the dancing, in truth, has some fascination and historical interest. What makes the film so amusing, however, is its enormously elaborate staging, its sometimes ludicrous dialogue, and its for-once-miscast genius, Peter Ustinov. He lumbers around first as Théophile Gautier, ballet critic, poet, and lover of women, and then as Sergei Diaghilev, impresario, egoist, and lover of men.

Not content merely to give Fracci the chance to dance, the participants in this project have loaded the tape with anecdotes and backstage gossip, trying to convey some sense of the vain and often malicious side of the ballet world.

It's a wonderfully outrageous idea, but it borders on inanity at times. Fracci seems radiantly unconcerned with the silliness of it all, and some of the dancing is quite fine.

This tape might be fun to watch with some friends, just for a laugh, but serious balletomanes should skip it.

■ *The Red Shoes*

Moira Shearer, Anton Walbrook, Robert Helpmann, Leonide Massine, Marius Goring. Written, produced and directed by Michael Powell and Emeric Pressburger.

Paramount Home Video, color, 1948, 136 minutes.

One doesn't like to use the terms "classic" and "one of a kind" lightly, but they apply here. This odd, haunting tale by Hans Christian Andersen of a lovely, doomed ballerina who achieves fame through the manipulative workings of an evil impresario makes a memorable film. Much of it is in too bright color, and some of the dialogue is dated or stilted, but it has aged well and is still probably the most interesting film about ballet ever made.

The plot is enough to interest most people, and the dancing is spectacular. There are snippets of classical ballets, but the centerpiece is the title ballet itself, *The Red Shoes*. It is presented as a phantasmagoric, special-effects piece. Shearer, who became an international star as a result of this film, was a lovely, lithe dancer with a shy but glamorous air. Robert Helpmann dances here as well, as does Leonide Massine, who choreographed the ballet. Anton Walbrook is sinister as the impresario.

If you've never seen this film—ballet fan or not—it's time to remedy the situation.

THREE

CONCERTS ON VIDEOCASSETTE

Concerts
and Recitals

◼ Claudio Arrau: *The Emperor*

Beethoven: Piano Concerto no. 5 in E-flat. Claudio Arrau, pianist; Symphony Orchestra of the University of Chile, Victor Teveh, cond. Narrated by Martin Bookspan.

Kultur, color, 1987, 85 minutes.

This videocassette is actually three separate shows: a performance of Beethoven's *Emperor* Concerto, Martin Bookspan's narrative documentary about Arrau's life and music, and a concert given by Arrau in 1984 in his troubled homeland, Chile.

The Chilean performance took place in the Metropolitan Cathedral in Santiago with 5,000 in attendance and another 6,000 standing outside in the rain listening to loudspeakers. Arrau's playing is predictably glorious, particularly for a man of eighty-one. The minor fluffs in the first movement don't matter; there is extraordinary beauty here, and his phrasing remains more aristocratic than almost any other pianist's. The problem lies with the shabby leadership of conductor Victor Teveh, who manages to be a beat or two behind Arrau for much of the concerto and brings the orchestra in before Arrau has completed his first-movement cadenza.

The documentary section is interesting. An intelligent and articulate interviewee, Arrau talks about his early life (old photos and some films), his debut at the age of five (he had to wear additions on his shoes so that his feet could reach the pedals), his training in Berlin, the encouragement he received from his teacher, Herbert Krause, and his psychiatrist, Herbert Abrahamson, who helped Arrau once overcome a serious bout of depression.

But the most exciting part of this tape is the footage of his return to Chile, where Arrau is a national hero. Thousands were at the airport, people cheered his way through the streets, hopefuls violated a state curfew to buy tickets, and in the week following the concert over 3,000 young people signed up for piano lessons at the country's music schools and conservatories. Even if the tape in general is somewhat of a disappointment, this exhilarating reception and its aftermath are worth seeing.

The camera tends to focus almost entirely on the pianist's hands (Arrau was never much of a mover at the piano), and one wishes for more shots of the cathedral or of the audience's reactions. The stereo sound and picture quality are excellent.

■ Claudio Arrau: *The 80th Birthday Recital*

Beethoven: *Waldstein* and *Appassionata* sonatas; Debussy: Images, Book 1: "Reflets dans l'eau"; Liszt: Années de pélerinage: "Les jeux d'eau à la Villa d'Este"; Ballade no. 2 in B minor; Chopin: Scherzo no. 1 in B minor. Claudio Arrau, pianist.

Kultur, color, 1983, 111 minutes.

This recital, recorded on Arrau's eightieth birthday, took place in New York's Avery Fisher Hall. Arrau has always been a less extroverted performer than either Horowitz or Rubinstein (his two closest contemporaries), but he has his own place among lovers of the piano. This tape shows just how special Arrau is—and why.

Martin Bookspan is the narrator, and between musical selections we see photos, hear Arrau discuss (in charmingly halting English) the music and the performer's needs, and get a good overview of the man himself. Arrau the pianist can move from Beethoven to Debussy in one program without melodrama and with absolute authority—he is truly one of the century's keyboard giants.

The performances are not note-perfect, but his musicianship is never in question. The highlights are the Beethoven sonatas—never mind that they probably should be played a bit more quickly. The Debussy hits its mark, and the Chopin is liquid and lovely. And when Placido Domingo and a birthday cake finally appear and everyone sings "Happy Birthday," you'll know that you'll want to see this tape again.

■ Jascha Heifetz: *The Greatest Violinist of the Twentieth Century in Performance*

Bach: Chaconne; Bruch: *Scottish* Fantasy, op. 46; Debussy: "La Fille aux cheveux de lin"; Gershwin: "It Ain't Necessarily So";

Mozart: *Haffner* Serenade, K. 250: Rondo; Prokofiev: *The Love for Three Oranges:* March; Rachmaninoff: "Daisies." Jascha Heifetz, violinist. Brooks Smith, pianist. Orchestre National de France. Narrated by Francis Robinson. Directed by Kirk Browning.

VAI, black & white and color, 1971, 63 minutes.

The wonderful thing about legends in classical music is that they usually live up to their status. After Jascha Heifetz' performing career ended in the 1970s, he devoted himself to teaching in southern California, where he died in 1987. Did a quiet, comfortable retirement make him less of a musical legend? Not at all, as you'll find out by viewing this tape narrated by Francis Robinson, who is known for his long association with the Metropolitan Opera. Unfortunately, whether of Robinson's making or not, most of his brief commentary is largely concerned with trivialities. The opportunity is missed to explore with Heifetz his life as a student prodigy and a world-famous musician.

Heifetz is a perfectionist, and his technical bravura is astounding, if a bit disconcerting to those who prefer artists to be less detached and more passionate. The Debussy seems not to interest him except as a piece of exquisite fluff, and the Gershwin gives a feeling of inspired trendiness, but he plays both pieces matchlessly. The Bruch seems very special to him, and he is truly absorbed in it.

Heifetz was an extraordinary musician, and it would be a shame to be without this tape. Others may play in a flashier fashion, but his sound is still unsurpassed.

■ *Horowitz in London*

Vladimir Horowitz, pianist. Produced by John Vernon and Peter Gelb. Directed by Kirk Browning. Audio engineer, Graham Haines. Includes Scarlatti: Six Sonatas; Chopin: Polonaise-Fantasie in A-flat, op. 61, Ballade in G Minor, op. 23, and Waltz in A-flat, op. 69, no. 1 *(L'Adieu)*; Schumann: Scenes from Childhood, op. 15; Rachmaninov: Sonata no. 2 in B-flat Minor.

Sony, A BBC Production, color, 1982, 116 minutes.

Most of this program consists of a tape of Horowitz' first recital at London's Royal Festival Hall in May 1982, after an absence of thirty years.

The tape is noteworthy for two other reasons. First, American director

Kirk Browning keeps his cameras on Horowitz' hands most of the time the 77-year-old virtuoso is playing, enabling us to watch as the master prepares chords, attacks scales, and calibrates his finger movements in observing dynamics. Unlike many pianists, Horowitz holds his wrists low and rarely curves his fingers, and his rebound from *fortissimo* chords is minimal.

One of the few remaining exponents of nineteenth-century Russian piano technique, Horowitz inherited that pianistic foundation which enabled such virtuosi as Rachmaninov and others to communicate their art. Seeing how he creates his diamondlike tone is valuable to aspiring concert pianists and scholars alike.

The second noteworthy element is an intermission interview (taped elsewhere) in which Horowitz talks about his youth in Russia and tells a string of anecdotes about some of his legendary colleagues. Unfortunately, in discussing his formative influences, Horowitz confines most of his reveries to name-dropping and snippets of ancient gossip.

The musical performance itself is vintage Horowitz. His approach to the pieces is magisterial, the clarity of his ideas impeccable, his energy unflagging. You may want to watch this performance with the sound plugged into a stereo; the loud portions tend to vibrate annoyingly on ordinary TV equipment.

Otherwise, the complaints here are minor. See this tape for an important musical education and a grand two hours.

■ *Looking at Music with Adrian Marthaler, Vol. 1*

Bach: Brandenburg Concerto no. 2; Gershwin: *Rhapsody in Blue;* Honegger: Concertino for Piano and Orchestra; Saint-Saens: *Danse Macabre.* Ilana Vered, pianist. Basel Radio Symphony Orchestra, Matthias Bamert, cond. Created and directed by Adrian Marthaler.

VAI, 1987, black & white and color, 50 minutes.

It was bound to happen eventually: classical music videos. Swiss TV director Adrian Marthaler has a fine eye and sense of humor, and this fifty-minute program (dating from 1979 to 1984) is almost nonstop entertainment. It may not suit everyone's taste, but the musicians are given center stage and the music is well served.

The *Brandenburg* is performed in a very bare, high-tech setting; the orchestral tutti players are together and the soloists walk around alone, with the camera catching up to them at various points. It's effective and a lot of fun. Even better is the black-and-white rendering of *Rhapsody in Blue*, which isn't quite Art Deco but has a period feel nonetheless. It is obviously taking place in the 1980s (some people are seen watching the fine piano soloist Ilana Vered on TV) but gives a nod back to the 1920s, when the piece was new. The brass players, sitting in a circle in well-upholstered armchairs, are just one of many nice images.

The Honegger Concertino features a piccolo player sitting alone on the floor amid empty chairs, a view of the piano from above, and a view of the ensemble through the curves of two cellos. It's all a little too busy and self-conscious—perhaps a bit like the Concertino itself. The *Danse Macabre* is played for high comedy in an empty concert hall, with the conductor entering and leaving through the prompter's box. The solo violinist is outside the hall or at the bar, and other frivolities include the musicians' looking half-dead at the end.

The music is all very well performed, but one tends to look and not to listen—at least the first time through. At any rate, classical music videos are a good idea, as long as the music is not distorted or cheapened. Again, not for everyone's taste but definitely worth a look.

Concerts: Educational and Documentary Films

■ **Charles Ives:** *A Good Dissonance Like a Man*

Starring John Bottoms, Richard Ramos, Sandra Kingsbury, Louis Zorich. Produced and directed by T. W. Timreck. Director of photography, Peter Stein.

Home Vision, black & white and color, 1977, 60 minutes.

This is an apt title for this curious film biography. Charles Ives loved dissonance, finding a visceral beauty in it. He was, however, considerably ahead of his time. Born in 1874 in Danbury, Connecticut, where he spent most of his life, Ives strove all his life to take music beyond what he called the "familiar three triads of church music."

His efforts, according to this film, were uniformly rejected. In one scene, a congregation walks out on one of his chorales. In another, a celebrity violinist comes to his home to play his pieces but will not stay for dinner. Somewhat paradoxically, while his ideas were amazingly advanced, Ives's musical ideals were grounded on a proletarian view of a future in which "men will hear their own symphonies as they plow for their potatoes."

Under T. W. Timreck's low-key direction, John Bottoms plays Ives as a cantankerous but lovable eccentric who stuck stubbornly to his theory of dissonance as a means of expressing beauty. Timreck inserts stock footage of scenes from turn-of-the-century Connecticut and Yale football games into a mosaic that is at once biography, docudrama, and video tone poem. Unfortunately, none of the music is immediately identified, and the film fails to explore Ives's obsessive love for his bank clerk father—the local bandleader and Ives's first and most important musical influence.

The final scene is perhaps the most telling about Ives's inner and outer struggles with an indifferent world. Old, ill, and rejected by musicians of his day, he taps his cane on the hard earth as he hears in his mind's ear a fragment of his Second Symphony. A plane flies overhead. He hurls invective at the noisy contraption but keeps humming and tapping.

The film is more effective in setting a mood than in finding a rationale for Ives's antipathy to the music of his time or in defining him. If you are one of those who think Ives is an overrated composer, don't bother with this tape.

■ *A Composer's Notes: Philip Glass, The Making of Akhnaten*

A film by Michael Blackwood.

VAI, color, 1985, 87 minutes.

Philip Glass is probably today's best-known composer of serious music. He is among the handful of living composers who do not have to support themselves through teaching or writing advertising jingles. This happy situation, however, is relatively new even for Glass, who drove taxis and did odd jobs for years while composing music.

Today not only do all his compositions get performed, he has also become a frequent item in glossy magazines and an occasional guest on popular TV shows. He has also written an autobiography, and something of a film version of his life story can be seen in this tape.

The premise of the film is to watch, from the composer's vantage point, the unfolding creative process of making and producing an opera. The film also presents a collection of Glass's ideas about music and, specifically, what he is trying to accomplish in *Akhnaten*. This opera, the last in a trilogy that also comprises *Einstein on the Beach* and *Satyagraha*, is intended to embody his ideas about uniting theater and music into one work. Included are scenes of rehearsals at the Württemberg State Opera in Stuttgart and excerpts from the American opening at the Houston Grand Opera. A composer to be reckoned with, Glass is made all the more fascinating by his unexpectedly easygoing manner and unaffected way of explaining his often complicated views.

Blackwood does not avoid pointing out negative reactions to Glass's music, including the fact that musicians frequently find it hard to concentrate on his endlessly repetitive figures. A court order forces a Dutch orchestra to resume rehearsals after it had balked at playing an endless set of triplets; a conductor notes that some musicians fall asleep while

Composer Philip Glass during the preparations for premieres of *Akhnaten* in Stuttgart and Houston. Courtesy Video Artists International.

playing Glass's music, and a bass player is caught surreptitiously reading a magazine during a run-through of the score. Nonetheless, his music is played again and again by ensembles and opera companies—the true test of success. Critics may carp, but his public grows in size and devotion. Like or loathe his work, it's tough to dislike this soft-spoken, chain-smoking Pied Piper of minimalist music.

■ *Guitarra! The Guitar in Spain*

Julian Bream, guitar. Produced by Laurence Boulting, directed by Barrie Gavin.

Home Vision, color, 1985, four cassettes, 60 minutes each.

These eight programs (each tape contains two) were originally produced for RM Arts/Channel Four in England. The whole can be viewed as a splendid travelogue (Spain has never been shown off to greater advantage), a great teaching tool (we get the political, religious, artistic, and sociological history of Spain in addition to learning about the evolution of the Spanish guitar over the last four centuries), or simply a remarkable series of concerts by one of the world's finest classical guitarists. The narrator is Lyndon Brook—although Bream, too, tells us a great deal—and the script is intelligent and informative without ever resorting to pedantry. From the opening shot of a guitar being made by an old craftsman, we know we are in for something special, and the following four hours do not disappoint.

VOLUME 1, Part one: *The Golden Age*. This volume opens with a reading of García Lorca's poem, "The Guitar." Brook then tells us about the first guitar piece ever published in Spain, in Seville in 1546. Bream plays this work (by Alonso de Mudarra) and the other works on this program (by Don Luys Milán and Luis de Navarez), on the vihuela—a small, lute-like instrument—while seated in a tiled courtyard that radiates serenity. All of the pieces for vihuela are interesting—almost all of them are very fast and played with pinpoint accuracy. We see shots of the interior and exterior of Seville's magnificent cathedral, Toledo, and the alcazar of Segovia, while Bream plays and the narrator discusses how music connected the people and the court in the sixteenth century.

VOLUME 1, Part two: *The Baroque Guitar*. Opening on a square in Salamanca filled with mummers, fifes, and drums, this program concentrates on seventeenth-century Spain, "an empire built on blood and the Bible." A discussion of vihuelas and the baroque guitar, which Bream refers to as the "Rolls-Royce of ukeleles," is followed by an intricate piece by Santiago de Murcia. The musical highlight is Luigi Boccherini's *Fandango* for two guitars, both parts of which are performed by Bream through the use of trick photography and overdubbing.

VOLUME 2, Part three: *The Classical Heritage*. Music dominates this program: Fernando Sor's Sonata in D, Variations on a Theme by Mozart, and Dionysio Aguado's Rondo in A minor are expertly played by Bream, as we learn how music, art, and architecture were taking leave of the baroque and developing into classicism.

VOLUME 2, Part four: *The Transition to Romanticism*. This program contrasts, among other things, romantic music with flamenco. Bream is joined by the flamenco guitarist Paco Peña, and they discuss different sounds and techniques. The music is by Franciso Tárrega, best known for his theories about classical guitar playing; it was he who placed so much emphasis on the right hand and the ways in which the strings were to be plucked. The music also comprises other composers' works, mostly transcriptions, served up handsomely by Bream in a variety of settings.

VOLUME 3, Part five: *The Poetic Nationalist.* All of the music here is by Enrique Granados—we get a remarkable reading of his Maja de Goya intensified by close-ups of the great painter's work. The composer's Spanish Dances nos. 4 and 5 are accompanied by shots of some of the Spanish architect Antonio Gaudí's residential buildings in Barcelona, and Bream plays the Valsas Poéticas exquisitely.

VOLUME 3, Part six: *The Spirit of Spain.* Isaac Albéniz' tone poems from the *Iberia* cycle are featured here as we learn how music is transcribed from one instrument to another (all of the Albéniz pieces were composed for the piano).

VOLUME 4, Part seven: *The Twentieth Century—The Last of the Romantics.* Bream plays Manuel de Falla's guitar pieces, which brought the guitar into the twentieth century. Joaquin Turina's *Fandanguillo* is splendidly played while Bream sits in Barcelona's phantasmagoric Parc Güell (another of Gaudí's creations). The mood shifts with *Tiento* by Maurice Ohana, a strange, atonal work that plunges us into the horrors of the twentieth century. Black and white stills of the Spanish Civil War, slow-motion footage of a bullfight, and quotes from Lorca about the inevitability of death foster a somber, reflective mood.

VOLUME 4, Part eight: *The Guitar: A Final Evocation.* Bream is joined by Charles Groves, who conducts the Chamber Orchestra of Europe in a superb performance of Joaquin Rodrigo's Concierto de Aranjuez against some lovely shots of windmills, fields of poppies, and charming town squares. It is a fine conclusion to the series, showing how the guitar has evolved from a playful dance accompaniment to a world-class concert instrument.

A fount of knowledge, charm, and virtuosity, Bream moves smoothly through four centuries of music, adapting to each style without a sign of discomfort. The playing is so good, the music so interesting, and the visuals so breathtaking that there are no dull moments in these four hours.

Viewers may want to view the entire series or whatever cassette caters to their individual preferences. Each program (or two, since that is how they are packaged) can stand on its own. But for a complete picture, see the whole set.

■ *The Music of Man*

Yehudi Menuhin, violinist, conductor, host and narrator; written by Yehudi Menuhin and Curtis W. Davis with Charles Weir; directed by Richard Bocking and John Thomson.

Home Vision, color, 1987, eight cassettes, 60 minutes each.

This series of tapes takes days, weeks, even months to digest. Each episode has slightly too much detail for comfort, but the moment Yehudi Menuhin picks up his violin (which is often enough) we forgive all. Invariably enthusiastic yet dignified, he draws us painlessly into each element of his subject. The list of assisting performers reads like a *Who's Who* of music, and the series is beautifully filmed. Whether the visuals are of a backwoods African tribe, a twelfth-century monastery, early Christian mosaics, Venice, or Versailles, they provide a delicious smorgasbord of scenes. "This is not meant to be a complete history of music," Menuhin says. "That would be presumptuous." But it certainly comes very close.

VOLUME 1: *The Quiver of Life.*
"Sound and rhythm are our communication; we heard before we could see." In this fascinating introductory cassette, Menuhin shows that our very identity is expressed through music when he plays one of Bach's unaccompanied partitas to exemplify the composer's ordered view of the natural world.
Menuhin associates the need for rhythm with the rhythm of the surrounding universe. He takes us to the Kalahari region of southern Africa, showing how music binds a primitive, nomadic people and keeps their history alive. Prehistoric bone flutes and drums made of mastodon bones demonstrate that music preceded speech, in a tradition that has used other natural means of communication such as animal horns and seashells.
This cassette tends to be a bit technical, particularly when Menuhin discusses wind columns and the universality of the pentatonic scale. But these moments are few.

VOLUME 2: *The Flowering of Harmony.*
In this volume, Menuhin follows the movement that led to the development of harmony. He introduces us to the sounds of chanting Tibetan

monks; each voice so deep that it creates its own harmony. The effect is startling. We hear how yodeling is a form of singing in harmony; chanting at a bar mitzvah introduces a discussion of the Islamic influence on music; Ravi Shankar, the great Indian sitarist, explains Indian music and performs a duet with Menuhin.

Our host then traces the development of Western music through the medieval church and the troubadours. He discusses Guillaume de Machaut, who was the last troubadour and the first of the great European composers. Around 1500, a more elaborate system of notation and bar lines came into common usage, and the advent of printing enabled original music to travel intact. We hear examples of music by Palestrina and the two Gabrielis in Venice's San Marco. By the start of the sixteenth century, the use of instruments had begun to overturn the total dominance of the human voice. This cassette is masterly and informative, and even a novice will have little trouble grasping the concepts discussed.

VOLUME 3: *New Voices for Man.*

Gesualdo, Lully, Corelli (whose Sonata in D is played as an example of music that is halfway between notated and improvised), Monteverdi, Purcell, and Handel—these are just a few of the composers dealt with in this cassette. Menuhin chronicles the growing popularity of music as an idiom that crosses social boundaries, and discusses musical entertainment as a moneymaking concern. With the invention of opera, there developed a form of music that appealed to all classes.

The discussion then turns to the role of music in colonization and in the New World, with a segment about African tribal music and instruments and a chat with the president of Senegal.

The real highlight of this tape (with a fascinating detour for the flamenco guitar) is Menuhin's tribute to Stradivarius and Guarneri, the two great violin makers of Cremona. His history of their dominance is effective not only because of Menuhin's own performances on these priceless instruments but also because the intricacies of violin making will fascinate any music lover. Mezzo-soprano Maureen Forrester sings Dido's lament, "When I Am Laid in Earth" (from Purcell's *Dido and Aeneas),* and the tape ends with Handel's *Royal Fireworks Music.*

VOLUME 4. *The Age of the Composer.*

This tape at times threatens to become a Venetian travelogue, but we eventually realize that Menuhin is visually demonstrating the movement of musical influence from Italy to Germany in the late seventeenth century. As the musical influence changed, so did the primary instrument. The keyboard began to challenge the strings for supremacy. The church organ and the music of Bach, a combination of discipline and power, set the tone for the future.

Menuhin uses the third Brandenburg Concerto to show how the combination of many influences made up Bach's style. He compares a sculpture to a fugue, in which many different, beautiful melodies are played together in counterpoint. Menuhin then moves on to Mozart, the first free-lance composer, and conducts his Haffner Symphony.

The last section of this tape is concerned with Beethoven and Schubert and their contrasting approaches. The high point is Menuhin's superb performance of the slow movement of Beethoven's Violin Concerto, which takes place in a room filled with Henry Moore sculptures. The juxtaposition of the music and sculptures illustrates Menuhin's point that the early nineteenth century was the beginning of the age of subjective expression.

VOLUME 5. *The Age of the Individual.*

After a rather odd discussion of the left and right sides of the brain, Menuhin moves on to Berlioz, the father of the modern orchestra. The modern orchestra can be seen as a microcosm of society during the romantic era, paralleling the growth of cities with their size and multifarious sounds.

The late eighteenth and early nineteenth centuries brought an era of great change in how musicians saw themselves and their music. The first superstar musician was Paganini, whose mastery of the violin revolutionized the instrument's technique. He invented double harmonics and adapted guitar techniques to the violin—vividly demonstrated by Menuhin.

Menuhin then discusses the development of the grand piano, which superseded the violin as the principal solo instrument. He allies its development to the onset of industrialism: an age that needed a dominating, powerful voice. Not suprisingly, during this period music took on cultural and political themes, such as are found in the operas of Verdi and Wagner.

This tape tends to ramble a bit, but the music more than makes up for it.

VOLUME 6. *The Parting of the Ways.*

Beginning with a barbershop quartet, this segment charts the flow of musical vitality from western Europe to America, which has a long-standing tradition of mixing musical influences from its three major colonizers, the English, French, and Spanish. Their indigenous melodies would later mix with African rhythms and give rise to blues, gospel, and rock; ragtime and jazz would become America's cultural music. Pianos, present in many homes by the turn of the century, helped popularize music of all kinds, although the phonograph and film later turned many people into passive listeners.

Menuhin demonstrates how European music mirrored a growing fragmentation of society. As an example we see and hear Stravinsky's *Rite of Spring* (superbly danced by the Béjart Ballet), meant by its composer as "a warning and a challenge." The music of Webern, Mahler, and Strauss is also used to illustrate a disintegrating society.

VOLUME 7. *The Known and the Unknown.*

After an opening tribute to those artists who directly influenced Menuhin, such as the violinist Fritz Kreisler, Menuhin returns to the international music scene of the 1920s and 1930s.

Music was reaching more people through the proliferation of media, especially radio and the movies; Leopold Stokowski brought the Philadelphia Symphony to Hollywood, and Toscanini's NBC Symphony Orchestra broadcast on the radio. Kurt Weill's ability to capture European discontent in his songs and music, and Arnold Schoenberg's rejection of traditional harmony and use of the twelve-tone row, are ably discussed. Menuhin then introduces us to the American composer Aaron Copland, whose theories of music, and the effects of social influence on it, are both enlightening and entertaining.

Another high pont is Menuhin shown teaching a class and demonstrating that the teaching of music has remained the same throughout history. His playing of the Berg Violin Concerto is a superb finale to this hour.

VOLUME 8. *Sound or Unsound.*

The final volume largely consists of Menuhin's discussion of modern music up the present. He tends to jump too quickly from one image to another, but his point is well taken: some things are made to last and some are not. He later refers to some punk music as "pathetic and nasty"—one of his few negative statements on these tapes. His reaction is obviously visceral, and he neglects to explain the social movements behind punk and rock.

This tape contains an overview of modern popular music from Bing Crosby through Elvis Presley to the Beatles and Judy Collins. Electronic music is touched on, and Martha Graham, dancing the role of Jocasta, proves Menuhin's point about modern expressionism. The minimalist music of Steve Reich demonstrates another route taken by modern music.

There is a riveting discussion with the late pianist Glenn Gould, who ceased to give concerts in 1964 because he felt that he could not compete with his own recordings. We see Gould in the recording studio, manipulating the sound on the huge console along with audio engineers, and it seems that the future of music may indeed belong to the machine. Menuhin looks pained, but his later point is well taken: a special bond exists between live performer and audience, and music making is a natural, organic part of being human. This cassette, although it sometimes skips around confusingly, ties in with Menuhin's thoughts on music as stated in the first tape. We have come full circle.

In summary, the mass of information we are asked to absorb in these tapes is occasionally overwhelming but never boring. The more than 170 separate segments are not all equally interesting, but each is worth seeing. Menuhin, well known for his love of communicating in both words and music, is the perfect host.

The tapes are available separately, and the buyer may want to consider carefully before making a commitment to such an expensive and time-consuming project. But there is nothing else like it on the market, and each tape is meant to be studied and seen again and again. Parents and teachers will also find the series an excellent teaching tool for older children and teenagers.

■ *Ozawa*

A film by David Maysles, Albert Maysles, Susan Froemke, Deborah Dickson. Executive producer: Peter Gelb. With Seiji Ozawa, the Boston Symphony Orchestra, Rudolf Serkin, Yo-Yo Ma, Jessye Norman, Edith Wiens.

CAMI Video, Sony, color, 1985, 60 minutes.

In one of the few revealing moments in this documentary about the eminent Japanese conductor, Seiji Ozawa, we hear him advising an aspiring Japanese conductor, "To be a conductor, you must be able to ride out a wave. As a Japanese, you must ask if you have the resolve to be a lone wolf."

The film leaves no doubt that Ozawa had the stamina and patience to become the only Japanese musician in the current front rank of conductors. With typical modesty, he also acknowledges the help of Professor Saitoh in Japan and Leonard Bernstein and Herbert von Karajan in the West. "I was very lucky," he says repeatedly.

There must be more to becoming a renowned conductor than simply resolve, the best teachers, and luck. On the evidence of this film, however, we will have to take Ozawa at his word. Otherwise there's no clue to this complex man—everything in his busy life seems outwardly well-organized and properly balanced. Even his wife and two children know their place in Ozawa's order of things.

From this film, it is apparent that Ozawa prefers to remain hidden within his Japanese self while ostensibly revealing an exterior self in the European music he conducts. He will not—at least in public—reconcile this duality; if his two selves converge, it is strictly a private matter. Such reticence ultimately makes Ozawa, as a man and a musician, less interesting than he first appears.

Ozawa admires and reveres his three teachers but discloses almost nothing about what he learned from them. Nor does he have much to say about the colleagues who appear in the film, and they keep their thoughts about him unspoken, too. The viewer is left wanting to know far more about Ozawa and his creative processes than this tape offers. A frustrating experience.

■ The Story of the Symphony

The Royal Philharmonic Orchestra, André Previn, conductor. Written, produced, and directed by Herbert Chappell. André Previn, commentator. RM Arts/BBC coproduction.

Home Vision, color, 1984, six volumes, 90 minutes each.

Where did the symphony come from? How did it develop? Who were its leading exponents? These are some of the issues André Previn addresses in this series of programs, originally broadcast on BBC. The volumes are aimed at a general audience that has more curiosity than background in classical music. The approach is historical, beginning with the emergence of the symphony as a musical entity in the mid-eighteenth century, followed by its development through the next hundred years, and finishing with a look at its evolution in our own century. Except for the first volume, in which he discusses and performs Haydn and Mozart, Previn concentrates on one composer in each program. The choices are obvious: Beethoven, Berlioz, Brahms, Tchaikovsky, and Shostakovich—the predominant symphonic figures of the past two hundred years. After surveying the life and times of each composer, Previn conducts one of his major works in its entirety.

VOLUME I—Haydn/Mozart. Haydn: Symphony no. 87. Mozart: Symphony no. 39.

Until the mid-eighteenth century, the composer was little more than a servant at the courts of European princes. He was considered more an entertainer than an artist. Mannheim was the musical capital of Europe, and Josef Haydn was the chief court composer. In the 1780s, Haydn formed a close friendship with Mozart, who spent much of his brief life traveling from one princely court to another, selling his musical services to various noblemen, and living a feast-or-famine existence.

Previn skims the surface but he clearly outlines the growth and development of the symphony, and Mozart's and Haydn's contributions to this new musical form. Unfortunately, Previn neglects to compare their musical and stylistic differences. When conducting, he apparently does use reduced forces to match the smaller number of musicians used in Haydn's time; the use of modern instruments, however, does not allow us to realize the actual sound of an eighteenth-century performance. The Royal Philharmonic responds well to Previn's moderate tempi, and Previn gives concise, unfussy readings of both symphonies.

VOLUME II—Beethoven: Symphony no. 7 (with excerpts from Symphony no. 5).

At the end of the eighteenth century, the patronage on which musicians depended was being eroded, forcing many of them to go into business for themselves, so to speak. Beethoven, one of the first to do so, drove hard bargains with publishers, gave many public concerts, and also took in pupils.

Previn points out that Beethoven's ideas had their start in eighteenth-century musical concepts, and that he owed much to Haydn and Mozart. His originality lay in the way he transformed unremarkable raw material into great music: using the first movement of the Fifth Symphony, Previn demonstrates how the composer took a series of intervals and shaped them into a titanic structure. Moving on to the Seventh Symphony, he illustrates musically how Beethoven worked an Irish folk tune into the opening of the final movement. Previn's performance of the Seventh is tidy and competent, but lacks passion.

Herbert Chappell, who produced the series, may have been limited in the visual material available to him, but greater selectivity in highlighting various soloists would have illuminated Beethoven's scoring. Here he concentrates on the ensemble to the detriment of individual performers—just the opposite of his approach in Volume I.

VOLUME III—Berlioz: Symphonie Fantastique.

It was no secret that Berlioz idolized Beethoven. Nor was anything else much of a secret in the life and career of this moody, extravagantly gifted composer of the mid-nineteenth century. The two composers were hardly alike. While Beethoven endowed some of his works with programmatic subtitles, Berlioz made almost a fetish of it. Beethoven lived much in his imagination during his later years because of his deafness, but Berlioz lived a life of dreams and created a dreamworld in his works. Many were musical embodiments of stories, tableaux, and ideas. His most famous orchestral work, *Symphonie Fantastique*, has the descriptive subtitle "Episode in the Life of an Artist."

This video volume is devoted entirely to this great work. Previn recounts the symphony's genesis at great length, recounting Berlioz' love for an English actress. After relating the gossip surrounding this symphony, Previn examines its musical merits. Ironically, much of Berlioz' originality, says Previn, may have come from his inability to play the piano. Because he could not conceive melodic and harmonic progressions in terms of ten fingers, he could think much more easily in terms of orchestral color. (In fact, Berlioz was the author of the first treatise on modern orchestration, which is still in print.) Previn demonstrates some of the work's unusual effects—barking dogs, howling winds, and a bubbling witches' cauldron—conveyed by screeching woodwinds and violins played with the wooden part of the bow.

Chappell catches these effects, imaginatively using the camera to enhance our understanding of the work.

VOLUME IV—Brahms: Symphony no. 4.

Johannes Brahms was the source of great controversy during his lifetime. On the one hand, his music was reviled for being reactionary and stuffy; on the other hand, he was the hero of the anti-Wagnerians, the torchbearer of classical values.

This cassette, which contains the most detailed of Previn's treatments, includes a twenty-minute explanation of the concepts at work in Brahms's Fourth Symphony and illustrates how he achieves his singular effects in an orderly but supremely individual manner. Previn's analysis is rewarding to hear, especially when isolated sections of the orchestra play, but once again, it seems there is far more visual material at Herbert Chappell's disposal than he chooses to use. Repetitions of the same shots of Brahms become tiresome, but the Royal Philharmonic obviously relishes the symphony and plays with an appropriately thick texture that never degenerates into muddiness.

VOLUME V—Tchaikovsky: Symphony no. 6 (Pathétique).

If Brahms was the composer of "pure" unprogrammatic music, Tchaikovsky was the opposite. For good reason, movies have often cribbed themes from his Sixth Symphony, from Romeo and Juliet, and from his ballets in order to depict romantic interludes or scenes of emotional stress. According to Previn, his peculiar gift took the form of irresistible lyricism, steeped in deep emotion.

Previn devotes considerable time to describing the tormented composer's efforts to deny his homosexuality, a biographical fact that is particularly relevant to his Sixth Symphony. The composer died mysteriously nine days after its premiere—possibly by his own hand—and Previn sees the final movement as a desperate cry for help. He attributes the pervasive feeling of anguish in the symphony to Tchaikovsky's genius in creating mournful melodies that are repeated and reworked in the score for maximum effectiveness.

In an age that values musical restraint, the Pathétique has received some cool performances indeed. Previn's reading, too, is less emotional than one might expect from a composer-conductor with such a stylistic affinity to Tchaikovsky. The tempi are appropriate, and Previn draws some soulful playing from the strings. His rhythms in the slow final movement, however, tend to be maddeningly exact—death seems a dull conclusion rather than an inevitable, sad end. Nonetheless, the performance is moving and deftly balanced.

VOLUME VI—Shostakovich: Symphony no. 5 (with excerpts from Ralph Vaughan Williams' Symphony no. 5 and Roy Harris' Symphony no. 3).

In this final cassette, Previn chooses to play the Fifth Symphony of Shostakovich in its entirety. The Fifth Symphony, which brought Shostakovich back into Communist party favor in the late 1930s, was hailed then as a first-rate example of socialist music. Previn demonstrates how it is nothing of the sort and goes on to give a stirring performance with the Royal Philharmonic. The slow movement bristles with tension, and the allegedly optimistic finale is especially effective.

Prior to that, however, Previn offers a cursory survey of the fortunes of the symphony. With the rise of serialism and formal iconoclasm, the symphony underwent a reevaluation early in the century, and many composers feel it no longer is a valid form. Nonetheless, Previn selects British composer Ralph Vaughan Williams and American Roy Harris as two of the most gifted and committed symphonists. (Their music comes as a surprise—there is no listing of either on the box.) Previn's performances of the slow movement from Williams' Fifth Symphony and of Harris' Third Symphony clearly show that they brought the musical spirit of their respective countries to bear on the form. Previn, however, does not mention Sibelius or other twentieth-century symphonists of stature.

Throughout the six volumes, Previn remains a poised and quietly enthusiastic commentator. Relaxed yet authoritative, he covers an enormous amount of material. Much of the credit for that must go to Herbert Chappell, who wrote, produced, and directed the series. If he had a better visual sense, this series would have been even more successful.

Previn does not have Leonard Bernstein's vibrant enthusiasm, nor does he communicate as well. But he is a sage and attractive narrator, along the lines of Alistair Cooke and Martin Bookspan. His orchestra remains one of the world's finest, and listening to it is a pleasure. The cassettes are recorded in vivid stereo, but the balances are relatively intact and so the monaural sound is excellent as well.

Although not as visually interesting as some, the series remains an absorbing and rewarding entertainment and an excellent teaching tool.

■ *Toscanini, the Maestro: The Man Behind the Legend*

(Including Verdi: *Hymn of the Nations.*) Jan Peerce, tenor; Westminster College Choir, NBC Symphony Orchestra, Arturo Toscanini, cond. James Levine, host; Alexander Scourby, narrator.

VAI, black & white and color, 1985, 74 minutes.

"Toscanini's performances are more than beautiful. They are right," said the great conductor Otto Klemperer. Host James Levine refers to Toscanini as "the most consistently great conductor of our century," and not many people would argue the point. A foe of sloppiness and misinterpretation, Toscanini conducted, and demanded to hear, precisely what the composer wrote. His approach was not without controversy, but none is included here. What we get in this video, rather, is endless praise, some interesting reminiscences by singers and other colleagues, and home movies of the maestro with the likes of Andrés Segovia, Vladimir Horowitz, and Gian Carlo Menotti.

There is much about Toscanini's refusal to conduct in his beloved native Italy while Mussolini was in power, his notorious affair with opera singer Geraldine Farrar, and his wild outbursts against unmusical or unprepared musicians. What is missing is his actual music making—apparently NBC refused to make his films with the NBC Symphony Orchestra available to the producers of this tape.

We do get to see and hear a complete performance of Verdi's *Hymn of the Nations*, filmed in New York in December 1943. Though hardly one of Verdi's greatest works, it allows us to view Toscanini in his element, splendidly conducting a great orchestra. This piece makes one long for more music and less gossip. A musical film more than an hour long that contains only a few minutes of music is an odd offering indeed. It's worth seeing once but is of no lasting interest.

Appendix
Production Companies
and Distributors

If any videocassette in this book is unavailable from your local video outlet, it can, in most cases, be ordered directly from the company. The following companies are cited herein:

CORINTH VIDEO
34 Gansevoort Street
New York, NY 10014
212-463-0305

EUROPEAN VIDEO DISTRIBUTORS
P.O. Box 7131
Burbank, CA 91505-7131
818-848-5902

HBO VIDEO
800-826-8282

HOME VISION
P.O. Box 800
Concord, MA 01742
800-262-8600

KULTUR
121 Highway 36
West Long Branch, NJ 07764
800-4-KULTUR

LYRIC DISTRIBUTION
P.O. Box 235
Roslyn Heights, NY 11577
800-777-5444

PARAMOUNT HOME VIDEO
5555 Melrose Avenue
Los Angeles, CA 90038-3197
213-468-5000

RCA/COLUMBIA HOME VIDEO
2901 West Alameda Avenue
Burbank, CA 91505
818-954-4950

SONY VIDEO SOFTWARE
1700 Broadway
New York, NY 10019
212-757-4990

VIDEO ARTISTS INTERNATIONAL
P.O. Box 153, Ansonia Station
New York, NY 10023
800-338-2566

VIEW VIDEO
34 East 23rd Street
New York, NY 10010
212-674-5550

Index

201